# *Bridging Cultures*

## Teacher Education Module

# *Bridging Cultures*

## Teacher Education Module

## Carrie Rothstein-Fisch

**LEA**

LAWRENCE ERLBAUM ASSOCIATES, INC., PUBLISHERS

2003    Mahwah, New Jersey                                      London

Camera-ready copy for this book was provided by the author.

WestEd

Lawrence Erlbaum Associates, Inc., Publishers
10 Industrial Avenue
Mahwah, NJ  07430

Cover design by Kathryn Houghtaling Lacey

**Library of Congress Cataloging-in-Publication Data**

Rothstein-Fisch, Carrie.
    Bridging cultures : teaching education module / Carrie Rothstein-Fisch.
        p.  cm.
Includes bibliographical references and index.
ISBN 0-8058-4207-1 (alk. paper)
    1. Teachers—Training of—United Sates  2. Multicultural education—United States  3. Home and school—United Sates    I. Title.

LB1715 .R59 2003
370'.71—dc21
                                                                2002026350
                                                                CIP

Books published by Lawrence Erlbaum Associates are printed on acid-free paper, and their bindings are chosen for strength and durability.

Printed in the United States of America
10  9  8  7  6  5  4  3  2  1

# TABLE OF CONTENTS

Preface     ix

   Organization of the *Module*     xi

   *Readings for the Bridging Cultures Teacher Education Module*     xii

   Acknowledgments     xiii

Chapter 1    Introduction to *Bridging Cultures*     1

   Culture and Education     1

   What is the *Bridging Cultures Project*?     1

   Validity of the *Bridging Cultures* Framework and *Module*     4

   Cultural Caveats     5

Chapter 2    Facilitator's Script     7

   Overview     7

   Objectives     7

   Optimal Use of the *Module*     8

   Learning to Bridge Cultures Takes Time     8

   Creating Trust and a Sense of Safety     9

   Many Ways of Learning     10

   Guide to Using the Script     10

      Presentation Tips     11

      Prepare the Materials     11

      Invite Others     11

      Check the Room and Equipment     12

   Use of the *Readings*     12

      Further Reading     13

      Connecting the *Readings* to Learning     13

   Script Introduction     15

   Jobs Scenario: Solving a Classroom Dilemma     17

   Description of Individualism and Collectivism     21

   Seven Sources of Home-School Conflict     26

      Independence versus Helpfulness     27

         Classroom Applications     27

      Personal Property versus Sharing     29

         Whose Blocks?     29

         Crayons in the Classroom     31

         Classroom Applications     33

Cognitive Skills and Objects Out of Context
  versus Social Skills and Objects in a Social Context   34
    How Would You Describe an Egg?   34
    Bridging Discourses of Home and School   35
    Classroom Applications   37
Child as an Individual versus Child as Part of the Family   38
    School Breakfast and School-Wide Cross-Cultural Misunderstanding   38
    Parent-Teacher Conference   42
    Classroom Applications   43
Parents' Role versus Teacher's Role   45
    Teachers Giving Parenting Advice   46
    Classroom Applications   47
Praise versus Criticism   48
    The Concept of "Burro"   49
    Mocking the Praise   49
    Rethinking Academic Award Activities   50
    Classroom Applications   51
Oral Expression versus Listening to Authority   52
    Checking for Understanding   53
    Guilt in the Principal's Office   54
    Classroom Applications   55
You Are the Bridge   57
Evaluation   59

Chapter 3   Effect of the *Module* on Pre-Service Teachers   61
The Course   61
*Bridging Cultures Module* Assessment Results   62
Evaluation 1 Exit Evaluation of the *Bridging Cultures Module*   63
Evaluation 2 Midterm Exam   68
Evaluation 3 Final Exam   71

Chapter 4   Overhead Transparency Masters   75
  1.  *Bridging Cultures* Workshop Agenda   77
  2.  The *Bridging Cultures Project* Initial Training   79
  3.  The *Bridging Cultures Project* Shifting Roles   81
  4.  Solving a Classroom Dilemma: The Jobs Scenario   83
  5.  Jobs Scenario: School One   85

6.  Jobs Scenario: School Two                                    87
7.  The Cost of Home-School Conflict                             89
8.  Individualism-Collectivism Features                         91
9.  Hofstede's Individualism Ratings                            93
10. Risk: Overgeneralizing                                      95
11. Benefit: Understanding                                      97
12. Seven Sources of Home-School Conflict                       99
13. Whose Blocks?                                              101
14. Crayons in the Classroom                                   103
15. Shared School Supplies                                     105
16. How Would You Describe an Egg?                             107
17. Science from Stories                                       109
18. School Breakfast                                           111
19. School Sign                                                113
20. School Letter                                              115
21. Parents' Role versus Teacher's Role                       117
22. Group Homework Practice                                    119
23. Praise versus Criticism                                    121
24. Oral Expression Versus Respect for Authority              123
25. Guilt in the Principal's Office                            125
26. You Are the Bridge                                         127

Chapter 5   Handout Templates                                  129
1.  Solving a Classroom Dilemma: The Jobs Scenario            131
2.  Seven Sources of Home-School Conflict                     133
3.  You Are the Bridge                                        141
4.  *Bridging Cultures Teacher Education Module* Evaluation   143

Appendices                                                     147
1.  *Bridging Cultures* Project Participants                  149
2.  The Hofstede Study and Expanded Data Set                  151

References                                                     153

Author Index                                                   157

# Preface

The *Bridging Cultures Project*, on which this *Teacher Education Module* is based, is an outgrowth of empirical research that demonstrated how differences in cultural value systems lead to conflicts in classrooms. These differences, which tend to be invisible, were shown to cause conflict between immigrant Latino families and the schools that serve them (Greenfield, Quiroz, & Raeff, 2000; Raeff, Greenfield, & Quiroz, 2000). In brief, schools tend to reflect the values of the so–called mainstream, which are highly individualistic—teaching students to become independent and take care of their own needs. In contrast, immigrant Latino families tend to be collectivistic—teaching children to be interdependent with others and to attend to the needs of the family. Although these are broad generalizations that do not apply in all situations, they help us understand why many students and their families come into conflict with schooling in the United States. Lacking knowledge of culture–based value systems, educators often misdiagnose classroom management problems or misinterpret parental behaviors. My

colleagues in the *Bridging Cultures Project* and I believe that conflicts between these underlying value systems must be considered if we are to improve schooling for a significant number of our students.

Acting on this belief, the *Bridging Cultures Project* researchers joined with teachers of immigrant Latino students in the greater Los Angeles area to explore the usefulness of a framework based on individualism and collectivism for improving schooling. The staff researchers included Patricia Greenfield and her student, Blanca Quiroz[1], both from University of California, Los Angeles (UCLA); Elise Trumbull from WestEd (a regional educational laboratory located in San Francisco); and me, Carrie Rothstein–Fisch, an educational psychologist and teacher–educator from California State University, Northridge (CSUN). Seven bilingual elementary school teachers completed the team. They were Marie Altchech, Catherine Daley, Kathryn Eyler, Elvia

---

[1]Ms. Quiroz is currently a doctoral student at Harvard.

Hernandez, Giancarlo Mercado, Amada Pérez, and Pearl Saitzyk.

In the fall of 1996, the staff researchers conducted a series of three half–day workshops to introduce the framework of individualism and collectivism to the teachers and share what had been learned from related classroom research. We asked the teachers to use the framework as a basis for observation first and then as a catalyst for change in their own classrooms. At the conclusion of the three initial workshops, the teachers shifted in their roles from teacher–participants to teacher–researchers. Over the course of the next four years, the team of staff researchers and teacher–researchers met every two to three months to share observations, innovations, and reflections, deepening our understanding of how culture operates in the classroom. Because the *Project* is truly collaborative, much of what is included in this *Module* represents the thinking of my colleagues, and therefore I often use the pronoun "we" instead of "I," although I am sole author of this publication, and I am responsible for any omissions or errors.

The *Module* focuses on immigrant Latinos because the empirical research on which the *Project* is based was conducted with that group. In addition, this population represents a large group of newcomers to the U.S., and applied research related to Latinos could be of great interest to many educators and families.

To understand any culture, it is important to study that specific culture; otherwise, programmatic innovations designed for students and families may turn out to be inappropriate. *Module* participants from Latino cultures have validated the framework of individualism and collectivism through their stories of conflict and confusion. However, immigrant Latinos are not a homogeneous group. Some immigrated from urban

communities or had extensive formal education in their homeland, experiences likely to make for fewer conflicts with mainstream schooling. Likewise, understanding students' cultures requires simultaneous examination of the mainstream culture if improvements are to be made in curriculum and instruction (Finkelstein, Pickert, Mahoney, & Barry, 1998).

Non–Latino cultural groups have also expressed epiphanies based on learning the framework's concepts. For example, following the *Module* presentation, many of my Korean American students have commented, "You just described my life!" The case of African Americans is more complex. According to Hale–Benson (1986) and Ladson–Billings (1994), elements of collectivism, expressed in students' preferences for learning in groups (versus in isolation) and a sense of family responsibility, are common among African Americans. However, their valuing of individual performance and competition with peers contrasts somewhat with the orientation of some other groups that have been described as collectivistic. Other parallels between immigrants in general and some African Americans have to do with conflicts they may encounter in the discourse norms of classrooms, in which there are expectations for separating academic language and content from personal values, feelings, and experiences. Specific information about how individualism and collectivism play out among Native Americans, African Americans, and Asian Americans can be found in Greenfield and Cocking's (1994) *Cross Cultural Roots of Minority Child Development*.

Because I saw the usefulness of the individualism and collectivism framework for the *Bridging Cultures* teachers as a vehicle for examining cultural issues in classrooms and schools, I began to present it to my students at CSUN. In the fall of 1997, I developed a three–hour instructional module that I used in my educational psychology courses geared toward preservice teachers. The *Bridging Cultures Teacher Education Module* has grown out of this initial form, refined over the years on the basis of student evaluations and my own experiences presenting the framework. An earlier version, titled *Bridging Cultures: A Pre–Service Teacher Preparation Module* (Rothstein–Fisch, 1998), was printed in draft form by WestEd and has been shared with many teacher educators and professional development specialists. The initial version allowed our peers to validate the content and processes of the *Module*.

The current *Module* is appropriate for teacher–educators to use in one or two class sessions and can be incorporated in courses in educational psychology, child development, counseling psychology, and any others that deal with culture in education. For example, I have used it successfully in a wide range of courses such as Psychological Foundations K–12, Issues and Theories in Early Childhood Education, Advanced Psychological Foundations of Education (a requirement for School Counseling students), and Applied Child Development for Parent and Child Educators. In addition, the *Module* has been adapted for a large number of professional development workshops with early childhood educators, elementary and secondary teachers, school counselors, and administrators (Trumbull, Diaz–Meza, Hasan, & Rothstein–Fisch, 2001).

Although the *Module* has been used primarily as a stand–alone training entity, the concepts and examples can be taught in conjunction with other cultural diversity frameworks. As a case in point, the Southwest Educational Development Laboratory produced a comprehensive training guide, *Understanding the Cultural Contexts of Teaching and Learning: A Training Guide* (Guerra & Garcia, 2000), which included elements from an earlier draft of this *Module* as one of 11 training sessions. Their training guide incorporated additional compatible cultural dimensions such as power–distance and low– and high–context communication styles that seem allied to the individualism–collectivism framework. The framework of individualism and collectivism has also been incorporated into other diversity materials (Brislin & Yoshida, 1994; Gudykunst, 1994; Lustig & Koester, 1999; Singelis, 1998).

## Organization of the *Module*

The *Module* is intended to help teacher–educators or professional development specialists build knowledge based on individualism and collectivism and translate it into an effective presentation or set of presentations that engage their audiences. Chapter 1 discusses the role of culture in education and introduces the constructs of individualism and collectivism. It reports the effects of the *Bridging Cultures* professional development project on the seven teachers mentioned previously. Chapter 1 also provides a bird's–eye view of the kind of effects the *Bridging Cultures Project* has had, something you may want to think about in advance.

Chapter 2 provides the actual training resources including an outline, agenda, and script. As the main body of the *Module*, Chapter 2 has several important features. First, the overview offers specific learning objectives for participants to accomplish by the end of the session. Second, it describes optimal uses for the *Module*, including setting the stage with essential skills for diversity training, preparation of materials, and a guide to using the script.

The largest component of Chapter 2 is a three–hour script. It is not intended for verbatim reading, but it does offer a specific example of how I have presented the *Module*. The script is designed as a lecture–discussion, with some structured opportunities for guided dialogue and small group interaction. Throughout the script, Facilitator's Notes are found in the margins. These are suggested as a result of my experience presenting the *Module*, including cues for overhead transparency use or places to stop for discussion. Of course, if facilitators are experienced in presenting material on multicultural education, they may find some of my suggestions obvious or unnecessary. I simply wanted to share my own experiences in using the *Module*. Oversized margins are intended to encourage integration of the facilitator's personal experiences and stories (and those learned from audiences) in the presentation and adaptation of the *Module*. Finally, Chapter 2 offers ideas for incorporating the *Readings for the Bridging Cultures Teacher Education Module* (described in the next section) into the presentation.

Chapter 3 presents the evaluation of a slightly earlier version of the *Module* used with preservice teachers (Rothstein–Fisch, 1998). I provide evaluation results of the *Module* from two sections of the same course (Psychological Foundations K–12) in 1997 at CSUN to give the reader an idea of the range of impact one can expect to have in a three–hour session. Chapter 4 contains suggested overhead transparency masters, and Chapter 5 provides handout templates. Appendix 1 contains the list of *Bridging Cultures Project* participants. Appendix 2 describes individualism ratings from 50 countries based on a system designed by Hofstede (2001).

## Readings for the Bridging Cultures Teacher Education Module

The *Readings* that complement this *Module* include five previously published articles and one book chapter. Provided as background information to presenters, the *Readings* are also appropriate for use by education students or other audiences as an adjunct to the *Module*. Suggested uses of the *Readings* are described in Chapter 2, but they deserve some introduction here. The 16–page Knowledge Brief, *Bridging Cultures in Our Schools: New Approaches That Work* (Trumbull, Rothstein–Fisch, & Greenfield, 2000), is the work most closely aligned to the *Module* itself because it explains the framework of individualism and collectivism, the *Bridging Cultures Project*, and the Seven Points of Home–School Conflict that are identified in this *Module*. Two brief articles are also included, Bridging Cultures with Classroom Strategies (Rothstein–Fisch, Greenfield, & Trumbull, 1999) and Bridging Cultures with a Parent–Teacher Conference (Quiroz, Greenfield, & Altchech, 1999). They were originally published in *Educational Leadership* and describe teacher–constructed strategies that enhance learning and home–school communication. The fourth and fifth articles are the original research cited throughout this *Module* that provided the empirical basis for the *Bridging Cultures* framework: Cross–Cultural Conflict and Harmony in the Social Construction of the Child (Greenfield, Quiroz, & Raeff, 2000) and Conceptualizing Interpersonal Relationships in the Cultural Contexts of Individualism and Collectivism (Raeff, Greenfield, & Quiroz, 2000). The final selection in the *Readings* is the first chapter from *Cross–Cultural Roots of Minority Child Development* (Greenfield, 1994), Independence and Interdependence as Developmental Scripts:

Implications for Theory, Research and Practice, wherein the constructs of independence (individualism) and interdependence (collectivism) are portrayed as developmental scripts with implications for theory, research, and practice. All six works contained in the *Readings* are published with the permission of their copyright holders (WestEd, Rothstein–Fisch, Quiroz, Wiley, and Lawrence Erlbaum Associates, Inc.).

## Acknowledgments

The *Bridging Cultures Project* is first and foremost a collaboration among colleagues dedicated to improving education for immigrant students, their teachers, families, and schools. What began as a relatively simple experiment to validate the usefulness of a framework for understanding culture became a partnership among seven elementary school teachers, four staff researchers, and more recently a cadre of about 15 students from the Michael D. Eisner College of Education at CSUN and the Psychology Department at UCLA. Together, we have shared stories of frustration with institutions and policies that seemed to derail student success, such as the virtual elimination of bilingual education in California, as well as successes resulting from applications of the individualism and collectivism framework. We have also shared our lives: new babies, illnesses, promotions, marriages, and countless meals.

Each member of the team deserves special thanks. Dr. Patricia Greenfield, whose theoretical model initiated the project, has served as our principal investigator, offering guidance, wisdom, and insight throughout. She has been a significant contributor to the thinking represented in this *Module* and all the *Bridging Cultures* activities and publications. Blanca Quiroz began the project as a

UCLA undergraduate struggling with the disharmony of being an immigrant Latina parent in a culture very different from the one she had known growing up in Mexico. Her stories of cultural conflict, many included in this *Module*, provided real life experiences that exemplify the constructs of the *Bridging Cultures* framework. Blanca continues to inspire us as a doctoral student at Harvard. As the *Bridging Cultures Project* Director at WestEd, Dr. Elise Trumbull coordinated our activities and led many of our publication efforts. She has been an enthusiastic and steadfast champion of the *Project* through each stage of development from inception to the completion of the *Bridging Cultures Project's Five–Year Report* (2001, available on the Web at www.wested.org/bridging/BC_5yr_report.pdf) and beyond. Elise has also contributed significantly to the editing of this *Module*.

Our seven elementary school teachers (see Appendix 1) have been the heart of our process and products, and quite simply, without them there would have been no *Bridging Cultures Project*. They have provided rich examples of how understanding cultural values can improve classroom practices in a wide range of areas such as literacy, mathematics, and home–school relations. It is their experience and wisdom that fill many pages of this book. They continually inspire us with their teaching gifts, and we have learned from their experiences and interviews and most of all, from watching them work with students and families in their classrooms.

The vital role of the Culture and Language in Education (formerly Language and Cultural Diversity) Program directed by Dr. Sharon Nelson–Barber at WestEd (which provided five years of funding for *Bridging Cultures*) cannot be overstated. WestEd has published several reports and the widely distributed *Bridging Cultures in*

*Our Schools: New Approaches That Work* (Trumbull, Rothstein–Fisch, & Greenfield, 2000). WestEd is co–publisher with Lawrence Erlbaum Associates, Inc., of *Bridging Cultures between Home and School: A Guide for Teachers* (Trumbull, Rothstein–Fisch, Greenfield, & Quiroz, 2001) and this *Module*. Special thanks to Naomi Silverman, our patient, insightful, and supportive editor at Lawrence Erlbaum Associates, Inc., who championed this *Module* and was instrumental in the development and publication of the *Guide*.

Acknowledgment is given to the copyright holders who have allowed their works to be reproduced as overhead transparency masters. These include Wiley, Dr. Geert Hofstede, WestEd, the Association for Supervision and Curriculum Development, Teachers College Press, and the Russell Sage Foundation. I sincerely appreciate the photographs from J. Patrick Geary (Overhead 14) and Giancarlo Mercado (Overhead 18).

Special thanks to Erica Kica, Sarah Walhert, and Art Lizza who complete our production team at Lawrence Erlbaum Associates, Inc. Grateful acknowledgment is extended to Shernaz B. Garcia, University of Texas–Austin, for her insightful suggestions on an earlier draft, along with the suggestions from one anonymous reviewer. I especially appreciate the efforts of Cherry Elliott Alena, who brought her considerable talents as a critical reader and artist to the design and formatting of the *Module*.

I owe a debt of gratitude to the education students at CSUN. They have assisted me for four years while I tested various iterations of this *Module*. They have validated it in their work as preservice and inservice teachers, parent educators, school counselors, and career counselors. They have asked hard questions, filled out numerous evaluations, and used the *Bridging Cultures* framework as a source of their own original research. J. Patrick Geary, a former graduate student in school counseling, has been especially helpful in presenting, evaluating, and editing the *Module*.

I am grateful to my mother, Ethel Rothstein, daughter of immigrants, who as a young widow sacrificed so much for her children's education. Endless gratitude is owed to my husband, Dr. Bryan Fisch, and our two children, Ariana and Jonathan, for filling my life with endless joy and an ever–larger appreciation for our family's interdependence.

# *Chapter* 1

# Introduction to the *Bridging Cultures Project*

## Culture and Education

Large waves of recent immigrants from Mexico, Central and South America, the Middle East, and Asia have necessitated new ways of thinking about learning and teaching. However, most educators are not adequately prepared for the cultural mix which faces them, and they do not have adequate resources to help them understand underlying cultural values. Although it is highly useful for teachers to learn about all the cultures that make up their classrooms (Banks, 1997; Banks, 2001), accumulating the information necessary to understand their nuances can be daunting. A *Bridging Cultures* kindergarten teacher, Kathy Eyler, expressed her frustration, "I wanted to understand my students better so I started studying Mexican culture. Then I realized that the children in my class came from many distinct regions, each with different histories and traditions. I just knew I would never know enough. I had to give up trying" (Rothstein–Fisch, Greenfield, & Trumbull,

1999, p. 64). However, Kathy's frustration turned to understanding, action, and advocacy as a result of the *Bridging Cultures* Project.

## What is the *Bridging Cultures Project*?

The *Bridging Cultures Project* is a professional development project that has found ways to improve cross–cultural understanding in classrooms and schools. It is based on a series of empirical studies demonstrating that deep, invisible cultural values affect the ways teachers, parents, and students solve home– and school–based problems (Greenfield, Raeff, & Quiroz, 2000; Quiroz & Greenfield, forthcoming; Raeff, Greenfield, & Quiroz, 2000). The research focused on immigrant Latino families and the cultural values system that is common in Mexico and Central and South America, especially among the rural poor and those with limited access to formal education. These immigrants come to the United

States with a cultural value system called collectivism (Greenfield & Cocking, 1994; Triandis, 1989). Collectivism refers to a cluster of interrelated values that reflect a particular worldview and motivate a whole range of thoughts, beliefs, and behaviors. In this value system, children are seen as part of a family whose members are interdependent. Sharing and helping others are essential because the goal of collectivism is group–family interdependency. Collectivism is the culture of immigrants from many parts of the world. In fact, 70% of the world's cultures can be characterized as collectivistic (Triandis, 1989).

In contrast, mainstream schools in the U.S. foster individualism, a set of values associated with independence, self–expression, and personal achievement. Individualism stresses personal choice and autonomy. In this value system, children are seen as individuals who need to become independent of their families. In the *Bridging Cultures Project*, we have used a framework incorporating these two value orientations as a way to help teachers become aware of the deep meaning of culture and how it affects everything from how schools implement federal breakfast programs to how teachers approach literacy.

Initial research studies prompted the question, could teachers understand and apply the framework of individualism–collectivism to positively affect communication, instruction, and learning?

In the fall of 1996, we tested whether the *Bridging Cultures* framework of individualism and collectivism could be useful for teachers serving large populations of immigrant Latino children. Seven elementary school teachers (four Latino and three European American) in bilingual classes in the greater Los Angeles area participated with staff researchers from WestEd (a regional education laboratory); University of California, Los Angeles (UCLA); and California State University,

Northridge (CSUN) (see Appendix 1). The teachers were invited to attend three half–day workshops conducted by the staff researchers that would introduce them to the framework of individualism and collectivism. Pretest data revealed that the teachers were largely individualistic in their solutions to scenarios presenting home– and school–based problems. On the pretest, 85% of their responses were rated individualistic. At the end of the third workshop, teachers responded to another set of scenarios in a more balanced manner (50% collectivistic responses, 29% individualistic, and 21% a combination of individualistic and collectivistic) (Rothstein–Fisch, Trumbull, Quiroz, & Greenfield, 1997).

Pretest and posttest data and videotaped records from the three workshops demonstrated three changes in teachers' thinking about culture. The following quotations from the *Bridging Cultures* teachers indicate that:

1. Teachers understood children and their families in new ways that bridged home and school cultures.

I am much more aware of how strong[ly] the collectivistic model is ingrained in my Latino students and how strong[ly] the individualistic model is ingrained in our curriculum, teaching methods and society. *(Amada Pérez)*

I feel less isolated and more heartened. I'm more aware of my individualistic tendencies. I have made efforts to connect more with parents. Awareness of the model and the possibility of change is encouraging. *(Pearl Saitzyk)*

2. Teachers improved classroom activities by emphasizing meaningful collaboration among students.

My reading and math journal is going to be much more group oriented. *(Catherine Daley)*

In my classroom, I started being really conscious of the help*ers—not* just allowing it, encouraging it. It is a much different atmosphere. I can tell by the looks on their faces.
*(Kathy Eyler)*

3. Teachers used personal reflection about the role of culture in thinking, learning, acting, and communicating for themselves and others.

I think before I act or speak when dealing with conflict that may occur between students and also participate more from this perspective on a professional level at faulty meetings or just at lunch. *(Elvia Hernandez)*

I am more conscious of my perceptions and immediate reactions to others. *(Catherine Daley)*

At the conclusion of the third workshop, the teachers unanimously asked to continue their participation in the *Bridging Cultures* Project. They described the roles they would like to take.

Developing a team that can present together at schools. *(Marie Altchech)*

I'd like to continue to research, share my experiences, write and work on presenting at conferences and do in–service workshops in my district, county, state, country, and world. *(Amada Pérez)*

I would like to continue to be a participating member of this group and help in any way I can. *(Giancarlo Mercado)*

I'd be interested in developing materials for students and teachers, as well as informing parent groups. *(Elvia Hernandez)*

All of the teachers described the framework as vital to their ongoing understanding of students, families, and themselves. Although the staff researchers planned to document the changes teachers made as they attempted to address goals they had set for themselves, we could never have anticipated the teachers' enthusiasm to continue as a group and ultimately their commitment to leadership in developing innovations in their classrooms and schools. As researchers in their own classrooms, the teachers have created their own unique ways for operationalizing the framework to solve a wide variety of problems. Indeed, it is largely the teachers' innovations, drawn from the cultural strengths of students and their families, that are used throughout this *Module* to demonstrate how to reduce cross–cultural conflicts.

The teachers and staff researchers continue to document their applications of the individualism–collectivism framework in many ways. Together we have generated a variety of data sources:

• Videotapes of the 3 initial training workshops and the first group meeting thereafter

• Field notes from 24 semi–monthly meetings that yielded detailed documentation of the teachers' experiences using the framework

• Written surveys and reflections from the teachers at numerous times throughout the past 4 years

• Observations by staff researchers of all 7 teachers at least twice in their classrooms for several hours (in 1998 and in 1999)

• Intensive individual teacher interviews, each often lasting more than 2 hours

Teachers also took on the role of professional developers. Their efforts have included planning and presenting at local, state, and national conferences. They have integrated *Bridging Cultures* content into courses for intern teachers, critiqued publications, and contributed to professional development materials. Detailed documentation of the teachers' growth is contained in the *Bridging Cultures Project Five–Year Report, 1996–2000*

(Trumbull, Diaz–Meza, Hasan, & Rothstein–Fisch, 2001).

The framework of individualism and collectivism has proven useful because it generates insights and understandings that enable teachers to build cultural bridges between home and school (Trumbull, Rothstein–Fisch, Greenfield, & Quiroz, 2001). For example, teachers discovered that students' natural desire to help their classmates could yield improved multiplication test scores (Rothstein–Fisch, Greenfield & Trumbull, 1999). They also discovered that when a writing prompt was changed from something general ("Describe a favorite TV show") to something that includes the family ("Describe a TV show you like to watch with your family"), writing increased in length, detail, and sophistication of vocabulary because students seemed much more interested in describing the joy of sitting with their parents, siblings, and cousins watching television, noting in particular how each family member liked something different about his or her favorite show. Thus, understanding value systems through a simple two–part framework, has allowed teachers to look at students, parents, and themselves in new ways that promote learning (Trumbull, Diaz–Meza, Hasan, & Rothstein–Fisch, 2001; Trumbull, Rothstein–Fisch, Greenfield & Quiroz, 2001).

## Validity of the *Bridging Cultures* Framework and *Module*

The content validity of the framework is derived from several scholarly sources. The framework of independence (individualism) and interdependence (collectivism) has been applied to Native American roots (including conquered indigenous peoples of North America, including Mexico), African roots, and Asian roots (Green-field, 1994, included in *Readings for the Bridging Cultures Teacher Education Module* as Article 6; Greenfield & Cocking, 1994). Empirical studies include a series of videotaped, naturally occurring parent–teacher conferences (Greenfield, Quiroz, & Raeff, 2000, *Readings* Article 4) and a series of open–ended hypothetical scenarios solved by students, parents, and teachers at two schools, one serving European American families and the other immigrant Latino families (Raeff, Greenfield, & Quiroz, 2000, *Readings* Article 5). This body of research confirmed that the values and beliefs of schools can conflict with the values and beliefs of families, causing confusion, misunderstanding, and sometimes misguided punishment.

The *Module* also draws on two sources of process validity: The original longitudinal study with our seven teacher–collaborators and the evaluation data from students and participants in *Bridging Cultures* presentations. The impact of the framework on the teachers was the result of prolonged interaction and collaboration, and the data demonstrate how changes occurred in teachers' understanding and behavior toward Latino students and their families (Trumbull, Diaz–Meza, Hasan, & Rothstein–Fisch, 2001). It is clear that this type of ongoing professional development and dialogue is powerful and compelling, but it is also very time–consuming and expensive. Thus, the need arose for a more traditional type of workshop format despite the well–recognized limitations of short–term professional development.

Data from the first pilot testing of the *Module*, presented in Chapter 3, provide an account of how university students enrolled in a course on educational psychology increased their knowledge of cultural value systems. It would be hard to imagine that one class session would produce results comparable to the impact on our original seven teachers, and the long–term effects of the *Module* on education students have not been studied systematically. Pre–service teachers would not be able to make changes in classrooms in the same way our tenured and experienced group of seven teachers did because they are still in the role of apprentice. Nevertheless, students and participants in our workshops claim to have been affected by a single or short–term exposure to *Bridging Cultures* principles and examples (Trumbull, Diaz–Meza, Hasan, & Rothstein–Fisch, 2001).

## Cultural Caveats

Before moving further, it is critical to state an important caution. Although this *Module* often focuses on differences between individualism and collectivism, I do not mean to oversimplify or overgeneralize about groups of people. "Human experience is far too complex to fit neatly into any conceptual scheme. No society is all one thing or another" (Trumbull, Rothstein–Fisch, & Greenfield, 2000, p. 4). Because intracultural variation is so important, it is mentioned here as well as in the script in Chapter 2. There will always be diversity within any group even if the group members are all recent immigrants from the same state of Mexico. For example, socioeconomic status is a very powerful predictor of school success—more so than culture alone. Any multicultural education program should consider an array of variables that affect individual families whether the family is rural or urban, formally or informally educated, monolingual or bilingual. All of these factors affect the degree to which a family is individualistic or collectivistic. For example, urban life and higher levels of formal education tend to make people more individualistic.

Cultures—and people—change over time as they come into contact with each other and as their economic circumstances change. However, many child–rearing values persist over generations (Greenfield & Suzuki, 1998; Lambert, Hammers, & Frasure–Smith, 1979), and deeply held value systems are more resistant to change than surface aspects of culture such as eating habits or language. Thus, even as outward acculturation moves people toward an individualistic orientation, collectivistic values and child–rearing practices are likely to persist.

In many ways, the value orientation of collectivism is particularly robust among recent immigrants from rural and poor areas of Mexico and Central and South America, with a strong emphasis on the unity of the family. Thus, if the framework proved useful with this population—illuminating dramatic differences between school and home, generating ways to draw on students' strengths, and helping to avoid conflicts in the classroom—then future research could address how it might apply in settings where relations between home and school values were more subtle.

As we seek to build bridges between home and school cultures, we must not reduce complex individuals to simple categories; nevertheless, we cannot ignore the compelling influences of children's home culture on their education. "If we can remember that the framework is just a tool, a heuristic for helping us organize our observations and questions, we can avoid the pitfalls associated with categories" (Trumbull, Rothstein–Fisch, Greenfield, & Quiroz, 2001, p. 4). In the next chapter, a method for sharing this heuristic is presented as a three–hour training *Module*. It is hoped it will promote essential discussion about culture and education.

*Chapter*

# Facilitator's Script

## Overview

The *Bridging Cultures Module* was designed to help pre–service and in–service educators understand the role of culture in education and learning from the perspective of two differing cultural value systems, individualism and collectivism. It is especially well suited for teachers, but it has also been used for training school counselors and administrators as well. This chapter offers a script of how to present the *Bridging Cultures Project*. It is organized as a three–hour module wherein participants explore the differences between the values of school and the values of immigrant Latino families through a variety of classroom–based problems.

## Objectives

At the end of the *Module* presentation, participants will be able to:

• Recognize that all people have cultures and no one culture is inherently better than another

• Identify the features of individualism and collectivism

• Examine their own cultural orientation and identify the values of their family of origin

• Cite examples of home–school conflict deriving from differing cultural value systems

• Describe classroom–based strategies that apply individualistic and collectivistic values to help students achieve their full potential honoring both home and school cultures

## Optimal Use of the *Module*

Diversity training is complex, emotionally and cognitively. It is fraught with challenges for both presenters and their group participants. The first challenge is for leaders to consider their own personal cultural values. Self–awareness is a necessary part of being able to teach cross–culturally and to develop genuine, mutual relationships with people from differing cultural backgrounds (Derman–Sparks & Philips, 1997). Acquiring self–awareness with regard to culture is a dynamic process, and like all development it evolves and deepens over time. Reading widely about culture, race, language, and power will certainly help.

The companion book, *Readings for the Bridging Cultures Teacher Education Module*, provides an important adjunct to this *Module* and is briefly described in the Preface. It should be read prior to presenting the *Module*. I recommend that *Module* presenters read the articles in reverse order beginning with the theoretical chapter by Greenfield (1994, Article 6) because that sets the stage for the others. The Greenfield article also draws on examples from non–Latino groups so that presenters can be ready to answer questions about how the framework relates to other non–mainstream cultural groups. Articles 4 and 5 provide important background information on how the empirical data referred to throughout the *Module* were derived. The three articles that remain (Articles 1–3) are highly worthwhile because they apply directly to the actual *Bridging Cultures Project*. As indicated in the *Readings*, presenters are encouraged to read our other *Bridging Cultures* book, *Bridging Cultures between Home and School: A Guide for Teachers* (Trumbull, Rothstein–Fisch, et al., 2001) or browse the *Bridging Cultures Five–Year Report: 1996–2000* (2001) on the Web at http://

www.wested.org/bridging/BC_5yr_report.pdf. Numerous additional resources on diversity are contained in the references and are cited in the script itself as reference points for further reading.

There comes a point where we must admit we don't know everything, yet forge ahead to reduce cultural conflict. *Bridging Cultures* presenters are eagerly encouraged to learn as much as possible, but they should not be crippled by what they don't know. Rather, they should be open to reading, watching, asking, and learning from others in a respectful, nonjudgmental way. College students are willing to help their professors learn more about their home cultures, particularly when they sense a genuine interest. I always encourage students to contribute their experiences to the learning process in ways that are most culturally meaningful for students themselves. Inevitably, their stories have enriched my understanding and cross–cultural knowledge.

## Learning to Bridge Cultures Takes Time

It takes time for facilitators to develop knowledge of the literature on diversity and to draw from their own personal histories (and those of former audiences) to make meaning of the *Bridging Cultures* framework: They must also allow sufficient learning time for participants to do the same. Each audience brings with it different levels of exposure and experience in working with students from nondominant groups, particularly the immigrant Latino students who are the focus of the *Bridging Cultures Project*. As with any new set of concepts, it is best to situate this framework within the learners' own lived experiences with real world cultural conflicts and concerns. Participants will need time to see what applies to the individuals and groups they work with in school settings. The best learning moments come when previously obscure values and beliefs become clearer and can be examined purposefully. It is therefore ideal to allow for as much guided discussion time as possible.

The content and length of the *Bridging Cultures* presentation should be varied according to learners' needs. Although the script in this chapter is designed as a three–hour presentation, it is far better to spread this workshop over several sessions, noting applications of the individualism and collectivism framework to issues such as classroom management, parent empowerment, literacy, and science or other subject content areas. Ideally, the framework should be infused throughout an academic semester or, better yet, a whole teacher education curriculum. With regard to any kind of professional development or theoretical framework, time is needed to progress from basic awareness to understanding and then to action and advocacy. Time allocated for ongoing discussion definitely helps participants consider their own experiences as they reflect on and anticipate interactions with students, their students' families, school staff, and the wider community. If three hours are not available, there are two places in the script that can be abridged or eliminated. For example, several conflicts could be combined, such as those focused on objects (Conflicts 2 and 3) or oral expression (Conflicts 6 and 7). Another way to abridge the script would be to reduce the number of examples offered for each conflict or to truncate the detailed interpretations that follow each example.

## Creating Trust and a Sense of Safety

Establishing a trustworthy and safe environment is essential before beginning a training session or class. In an ongoing course, this is probably already established, but in a single workshop–style presentation, participants may feel vulnerable about sharing personal culture–based experiences, particularly if their cultures have a different value system from the mainstream. Discussions of cultural value systems may cause uneasiness or defensiveness. Therefore, it is wise to establish trust and safety rules before the presentation for optimal participation.

Trust is essential. First, facilitators must trust themselves. "The clearer the structure and the more secure you are in the role of facilitator, the better the chances for a safe climate and productive discussion" (Mesa–Bains & Shulman, 1994, p. 6). For instance, facilitators who trust themselves can reframe questions and draw on body language cues (Mesa–Bains & Shulman, 1994). Promoting trust within the audience means allowing for multiple ways of learning and contributing to the discussion, recognizing that some participants may want to make contributions orally whereas others are satisfied by listening and having opportunities to write responses. Private conversations with people who have been reluctant to share (such as prior to the presentation or during break time) build trust and establish the sentiment that all opinions are valued.

Ground rules are especially important to establish. The audience can be asked to generate their own list of ground rules about sharing, or the facilitator can bring a tentative list of suggested rules. For example, attentive, respectful, nonjudgmental listening to one speaker at a time is important because it eliminates interruptions. Establishing a code of confidentiality within the group so that personal disclosures are not shared beyond the session can also be an important ground rule to engender trust and group sharing.

Sometimes discussion of cultural conflicts can trigger heightened emotions. For example, college students may come to a realization about family conflicts and be in need of counseling services. In such cases, knowledge of referral resources can be helpful. In addition, some participants may feel that their values are "better" than others, and conflict resolution skills may be necessary. Girard and Koch (1996) suggested that conflicting interests be seen as a "shared problem, to be solved mutually" (p. 9). In this case, the goal is to understand each other without a judgment as to which cultural value system is better. Remind participants that both individualism and collectivism are important for school success and ask them to generate a list demonstrating that both systems contribute to learning in meaningful ways.

## Many Ways of Learning

Facilitators will find many participants gravitating toward the framework, eager to share stories of their personal experiences with individualism and collectivism. In contrast, some participants may be uncomfortable with personal narratives. One way to avoid the tensions caused when personal narratives become too time–consuming during discussion is to have people share in pairs or small groups. This fosters respect for participants' lived experiences while not requiring the whole group to become embroiled in what some may feel are tangential personal issues.

At the beginning and end of the *Module* presentation, there are opportunities for participants to write. These are included as handouts in Chap-

ter 5. The first one includes an informal response to a school–based scenario. The second handout, Seven Sources of Home–School Conflict, provides a vehicle for participants to write notes in an organized fashion during the discussion. Toward the end of the presentation, the audience is given Handout 3 and invited to conceptualize and illustrate a cultural bridge. Drawing an actual bridge allows participants to envision and personalize how they might become cultural conduits for students and families. Handout 4 is an evaluation of the *Module* that allows participants to reflect on their own experiences with individualism and collectivism while providing a critique of the presentation method and content. "No matter how coherently planned, sensibly constituted, or well led they may be, cultural education programs take on a life of their own when they are enacted" (Finkelstein, et al., 1998, p. 26). Hence, it is important to evaluate each presentation of the *Module* to learn the myriad ways in which it may be understood and experienced.

## Guide to Using the Script

There are two parts to the script. The narrative script is very close to how I actually present the *Module* in three hours. Remember that this is a sample script. Put the content in your own words and construct a learning experience that is geared to your unique audience. I use the script as a foundation and read several specific examples verbatim because they capture the original research well. First read the needs of the audience, then engage and alter the script.

The second part of the script is the Facilitator's Notes. These are included in the margins with suggestions and ideas for the process of presenting the *Module*, and they include discussion topics and indications for putting up overhead transparencies or distributing handouts. Reference citations found in the script are not necessarily intended to be read aloud; they are provided as a means to locate original sources. Most important, adapt the script to your own specifications, and plan how you will introduce, present, and evaluate key concepts and activities.

## Presentation Tips

Strategies for preparing to present new material are offered in this section. They may be so familiar to you that you want to skim past them. On the other hand, some of them may be good reminders or trigger thoughts of new strategies you can use. For example, I practice new material out loud to determine if there are points of confusion or words that trip me up. To overcome these problem areas, I recommend marking up the pages with your own margin notes or references. A highlighter will help to emphasize key points you don't want to miss if time runs short. Whenever possible, practice in front of a friendly audience to gather constructive comments before the actual presentation.

### Prepare the Materials

The *Module* has been perforated and hole–punched to facilitate its use. For example, you may wish to detach the pages in Chapters 4 and 5 for ease in dupilcating the overheads (onto transparency masters) and the handouts. Likewise, the script may be easily detached to make it less cumbersome in handling during the lecture–discussion. The punched holes make it easy to put the entire book into a three–ring binder. A binder is a good way to store the *Readings*, as well. Consider a binder as an expanding repository for other cultural diversity resources that complement the *Module*.

It probably goes without saying, but be sure you have more than enough handouts for the group you anticipate. These materials are copyrighted; therefore we have cited the full references, and they should remain printed on reproductions of the handouts. Prepare an agenda that outlines specifically what you plan to do or use the one included in Chapter 4 (Overhead 1). Develop an evaluation, using Handout 4 as a start: Ask the questions you would like answered. Bring blank overhead transparency sheets and marking pens for note-taking because writing down participants' responses to problems or questions can be helpful for learners. Taking time to record audience comments also demonstrates that their responses are valued, and the need for a visual focal point is satisfied. Finally, if you decide to write comments on blank overhead transparencies, you'll have a written reminder of the discussion content.

### Invite Others

If you are a college professor, consider advertising the *Bridging Cultures Module* as a workshop if you think others in addition to your students might be interested in attending. Of course, there are benefits and drawbacks to bringing others to the discussion. If you have a well–established trust level in the middle of a college course, you may not want the disruption outsiders may introduce. New participants may also change the established group's security. If you do decide to invite others, such as school–based personnel, be sure to give advance notice to them and the class. Provide clear directions and free parking if possible. Arrange for refreshments so that break times can be spent in the same room and the conversation can be informal but still purposeful.

## Check the Room and Equipment

The room should be large enough to allow a comfortable seat for each participant. Ideally, tables or desks should be arranged in a theater–style format for the initial part of the presentation and then moved into small clusters for group sharing time. Also, check for distractions such as uncomfortable room temperature and outside noises.

Be certain that the overhead projector is in good working order and that additional light bulbs are available just in case you need them. If the room is very large, you may need a microphone and speakers. Be cautious about cords and other distractions or obstacles that can impede your presentation. Many of these details may seem trivial, yet failure to deal with them can sabotage an otherwise excellent educational experience.

## Use of the *Readings*

The companion book, *Readings for the Bridging Cultures Teacher Education Module*, includes six articles associated with the *Module* that supplement it in two ways. First, they provide the full text of previously published works and are intended as important background knowledge for facilitators. Second, they are highly worthwhile resources for participants. They are introduced below along with comments about the intended audiences for each.

Article 1. Bridging Cultures in Our Schools: New Approaches That Work. Trumbull, E., Rothstein-Fisch, C., & Greenfield, P. M. (2000).

The first article is a widely distributed 16–page description of the framework of individualism and collectivism, the *Bridging Cultures Project*, and

the Seven Points of Home–School Conflict, including examples and strategies. Education students have commented that this article helped to solidify the concepts from the presentation and was useful in course assignments.

Article 2. Bridging Cultures with Classroom Strategies. Rothstein-Fisch, C., Greenfield, P. M., & Trumbull, E. (1999).

In a brief and concise manner, Article 2 provides an overview of the *Bridging Cultures Project* with commentary on specific classroom practices (many of which are included in this *Module*) such as the hummingbird example.

Article 3. Bridging Cultures with a Parent-teacher Conference. Quiroz, B., Greenfield, P. M., & Altchech, M. (1999).

The process of moving from a child–driven, individual parent–teacher conference toward group parent–teacher conferences is described in Article 3, including reflections from the teacher who made the changes.

Article 4. Cross-cultural Conflict and Harmony in the Social Construction of the Child. Greenfield, P. M., Quiroz, B., & Raeff, C. (2000).

Written primarily for scholars, Article 4 describes nine naturally occurring parent–teacher conferences between immigrant Latino parents and their children's European American elementary school teacher. Excerpts from this research are mentioned in the script. This article is highly recommended for professors, professional development specialists, or advanced education students.

Article 5. Conceptualizing Interpersonal Relationships in the Cultural Contexts of Individualism and Collectivism. Raeff, C., Greenfield, P. M., & Quiroz , B. (2000).

Fifth–grade children, their parents, and their teachers are offered a series of home–school conflcts and asked how to solve them in Article 5. The *Module* script begins with one scenario from this research, the classroom task of cleaning the chalkboard. Because this research is fundamental to the *Module*, it is highly recommended for professors and professional developmental specialists. Advanced education students might also find the original research very interesting.

Article 6. Independence and Interdependence as Developmental Scripts: Implications for Theory, Research, and Practice. Greenfield, P. M. (1994).

Article 6 is actually the first chapter of a book that explores the framework of independence (individualism) and interdependence (collectivism) related to people with American roots (including the indigenous people of America, now considered Mexican or Native American), African American roots, and Asian roots. The entire book is highly worthwhile. The chapter is included in the *Readings* primarily as background for *Module* preparation or for advanced students.

### Further Reading

As mentioned in the Preface, two additional resources are associated with the *Bridging Cultures Project*.

1. *Bridging Cultures between Home and School: A Guide for Teachers*. Trumbull, E., Rothstein–Fisch, C., Greenfield, P. M. & Quiroz, B. (2001).

The *Guide* describes the *Bridging Cultures Project* in some detail and includes chapters on cross–cultural communication, parent involvement, and teachers as researchers. It is a perfect complement to the *Module* since it contains many teacher–constructed strategies for promoting cul-

turally appropriate instruction.

2. The *Bridging Cultures Project Five–Year Report, 1996–2000*. Trumbull, E., Diaz–Meza, R., Hasan, A., & Rothstein–Fisch, C. (2001). On the Internet at http://www.wested.org/bridging/BC_5yr_report.pdf.

Serving as summary report of the *Bridging Cultures Project*, the *Five–Year Report* describes the training, follow–up, professional development meetings, research methods, outcomes, and future directions of the *Project*.

### Connecting the *Readings* to Learning

The selected *Readings* that complement this *Module* are ideal as sources for follow–up assignments if connected to part of an ongoing course. For example, teacher–education students could use the information contained in the *Readings* as a resource for writing papers, structured observations of multicultural classrooms, or preparing for essay exams on topics such as:

- The role of culture in education

- Families and schools

- Multicultural education—new trends and ideas

- Applying the principles of individualism and collectivism in the classroom

- Serving the needs of immigrant students

Because the *Readings* provide vivid examples of how culture influences learning and teaching, they are helpful as catalysts for reflective practice or as a guide for culturally meaningful observations of students, their teachers, and/or their families.

The *Module* has been designed so that the presentation precedes the distribution of the *Readings* in order to produce a "wow" effect when the graphs comparing responses from two differing cultural groups are shown the first time. However, in some cases it may be advisable to have participants prepare for the *Module* presentation by doing the reading first. Whenever the *Readings for the Bridging Cultures Teacher Education Module* are offered, learning more about individualism and collectivism helps deepen the understanding and appreciation of culture in schools.

SCRIPT                                          NOTES

## Introduction
*5 minutes*

Overhead 1
Agenda

Today we will learn about the *Bridging Cultures Project*. Here is what we will do. (*Overhead 1*) It's an ambitious agenda, so let's get started. The *Bridging Cultures Project* is part of an ongoing professional development action research project. It includes two phases.

| **Bridging Cultures Workshop Agenda** |
| --- |
| • Introduction to the *Bridging Cultures Project*<br>• Solving a Classroom Dilemma<br>• Description of the *Bridging Cultures* Framework<br>• The Seven Points of Home-School Conflict<br>• Break<br>• Envisioning the Cultural Bridge<br>• Questions and Applications<br>• Evaluation |

### Phase 1
### Initial training: Teachers as participants

(*Overhead 2*) In the fall of 1996, seven bilingual elementary school teachers came together at UCLA to learn more about the role of culture in education. Four of the teachers were Latino and three were European American. The teachers represented all elementary grade levels from kindergarten through fifth grade.

Overhead 2
*Bridging Cultures Project*

| **The *Bridging Cultures Project*** |
| --- |
| **Initial training, 1996**<br><br>Participants<br>    Seven bilingual Spanish-English elementary teachers<br>    (four Latino, three European American)<br><br>Method<br>    Three videotaped workshops over four months<br><br>Outcome<br>    All teachers learned to understand and apply<br>    the *Bridging Cultures* framework |

The three initial workshops lasted about four hours each and were conducted over a four month period. All sessions were videotaped, and the participants and researchers ate breakfast and lunch together. At the first meeting, the teachers took a pretest consisting of four problems to solve related to home and school cultural values. At the third meeting, they took a similar test to measure if their understanding and problem–solving skills related to culture had changed. All teachers had made a significant shift in understanding immigrant Latino children and families, even the Latino teachers! (Rothstein–Fisch, Trumbull, Quiroz, & Greenfield, 1997)

| NOTES | SCRIPT |
|---|---|

**Phase 2**
**Shifting the teachers' role from participant to researcher and disseminating the research**

At the third and final meeting, the teachers requested that the meetings continue. As one teacher recalled:

> I remember saying that we would continue to meet and continue to dialogue and then try to teach others what we had learned. We were willing to do whatever it took to continue. The thing that was amazing to me was that it was a total commitment, 100% consensus! (*Amada Pérez*) (Rothstein-Fisch, 2000.)

Overhead 3
*Bridging Cultures Project*

---

**The *Bridging Cultures Project***

**Shifting roles, 1997 - 2001**

Bi-monthly meetings provided opportunities to continue applying and researching the framework

Teachers moved from being teacher-participants to teacher-researchers, finding new examples and applications of *Bridging Cultures* in their schools

Teachers became conference presenters, publication co-authors, and school leaders

Overhead 3

---

(*Overhead 3*) After the initial three meetings, teachers moved from the role of teacher–participant to teacher–researcher as they continued to find new ways to explore, learn, and apply the *Bridging Cultures* framework. Phase 2 continues with an expanded group of other educators and graduate students who are focusing their research on *Bridging Cultures*.

If participants have read the articles from the *Readings* prior to the presentation, the description of the *Project* and the participants could be posed as questions to the audience. For example, "Who remembers something about the participants in the *Bridging Cultures Project?*" The *Readings* can also be mentioned with regard to the *Project*'s dissemination component.

In addition, the *Project* has been widely disseminated. The *Bridging Cultures Project* has been presented more than 100 times between 1997 and 2001 by the staff researchers, the initial teacher–participants, and graduate students. In addition, the teachers have become co–authors of articles and are considered school leaders in many ways.

SCRIPT

NOTES

## Jobs Scenario:
## Solving a Classroom Dilemma
*20 minutes*

(*Overhead 4, Handout 1*) This Jobs Scenario was used as part of a series of studies (Raeff, et al., 2000) in which parents, teachers, and fifth–grade students from two Los Angeles schools were asked to resolve conflicts centered around home and school themes. (A scenario is a vignette demonstrating how differing value orientations lead to different inter- pretations of the same event or to different behav- iors in the same circumstances.) Take a minute to respond to this scenario.

Overhead 4
Solving a Classroom Dilemma:
The Jobs Scenario

> **Solving a Classroom Dilemma**
>
> **The Jobs Scenario**
>
> It is the end of the school day, and the class is cleaning up. Salvador isn't feeling well, and he asks Emanuel to help him with his job for the day, which is cleaning the blackboard. Emanuel isn't sure that he will have time to do both jobs.
>
> **What do you think the teacher should do?**
>
> Overhead 4

Handout 1
Solving a Classroom Dilemma:
The Jobs Scenario

1. Put up Overhead 4 and/or distribute Hand- out 1. Ask participants to write responses.

2. Share answers in whole group or pairs. Cap- ture comments on blank overhead or chalk- board.

3. Focus debriefing on:
- Finding a third person, either the teacher or another student (individalistic)
- Protecting the task, focusing on task completion (individualistic)
- The element of choice, Emanuel's choice to help or not (individualistic)
- Helping automatically without questioning (collectivistic)
- Helping without concern for personal preference or job (collectivistic)

4. Participants may ask, "How do we know Salvador is really sick?" or "r "Whthis the teacher's problem?" These responses represent an individualistic perspective: Help isn't offered unless the situation is desperate or it is convenient to do so. These points may be discussed during the school graphs debriefing.

NOTES

SCRIPT

Let's see how parents, teachers, and fifth–grade students in two different schools responded to the same scenario.

Overhead 5
The Jobs Scenario: School One

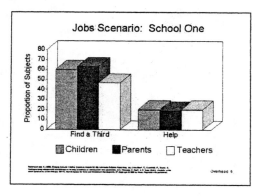

Let participants notice that the predominant response of the parents is to help, while the teachers and children have different responses.

(*Overhead 5*) The parents and children sampled in School One were entirely European American and the teachers were of mixed ethnicity. From the graph, we can see that the dominant response was that the teacher should find a third person to clean the blackboard. In fact, parents, children, and their teachers overwhelmingly preferred this solution to the dilemma. Participants reasoned that Emanuel had his own job to do and that his first responsibility would be to that task. This response illustrates the value of independence, not infringing on others' rights. Some said that the third party should be a volunteer; this response illustrates a value placed on choice, in this case, the choice of whether or not to help. It also emphasizes the importance of getting the job done, an orientation toward accomplishing a task rather than focusing on the needs of a sick friend who may need help. Notice that there is a general agreement among children, parents, and teachers about how to resolve this dilemma.

Overhead 6
The Jobs Scenario: School Two

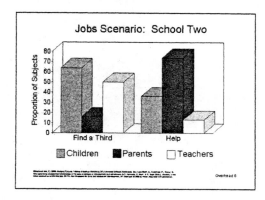

(*Overhead 6*) Now, let's take a look at School Two. School Two served a population that was entirely Latino. The teachers were again of mixed ethnicity (proportionate to School One). Looking at the graph of School Two, what do you notice?

| SCRIPT | NOTES |
|---|---|

Immigrant Latino parents solved the jobs dilemma by overwhelmingly (80%) selecting a helping response. They believed that when a group member such as a fellow student needs help, it should be provided automatically. The parents' response contrasts with the responses of the students and teachers. The teachers in School Two responded very much the same as the teachers in School One. Most students agreed with the position of their teachers, but a significant minority agreed with the values of their parents. Thus, a simple classroom job, cleaning the chalkboard, can reveal two completely different views of human relations.

(*Overheads 5 & 6*) Notice that there is harmony between the students, parents, and teachers in School One: The pattern of responses is more or less the same for parents, teachers, and students. This contrasts with the disharmony of School Two, where students were pulled between two sets of cultural values. The graph of School Two also reveals that the conflict is often resolved in favor of the school, thus invalidating parents' developmental goals for their children.

Alternate between Overheads 5 & 6, the graphs of School One and School Two, one after the other. Ask participants if they see a pattern.

Consider how hard it is for students to be wrenched between the values at home and the values at school because they are in direct conflict. These deep and often invisible cultural value differences cause all kinds of differences and conflicts in motivation, learning, and education, as we will see.

| NOTES | SCRIPT |
|---|---|

### The Cost of Home–School Conflict

Overhead 7
The Cost of Home–School Conflict

(*Overhead 7*) One of our *Bridging Cultures* teachers, an immigrant Latina, described the conflict poignantly. This is an experience very common for immigrant children and their families.

---

**The Cost of Home-School Conflict**

"[We came to feel that] the rules at school were more important than the rules at home. The school and the teachers were right. As a child, you begin to feel the conflict. Many of my brothers stopped communicating with the family and with my father because he was ignorant."

Amada Irma Pérez
Third-Grade Teacher

Overhead 7

---

Remember that some parents, teachers, and students at the predominantly European American school (One) were also in favor of the student helping a classmate in the Jobs Scenario but only about 20% of the time. Thus, while one type of response is clearly preferred, variations in beliefs about independence and helpfulness exist within any population. Likewise, in the school with Latino children and parents (Two), about 10% of the parents selected the response to "find a third person." The children were torn in their responses, wanting to solve the classroom job dilemma by helping (about 30%) much more often than their teachers (about 10%), but less frequently than their parents (about 70%).

| SCRIPT | NOTES |
|--------|-------|

## Description of
## Individualism and Collectivism
*25 minutes*

Studies such as the one just described grew out of new ways of thinking about cultural values in education. The *Bridging Cultures Project* focuses on the cultural dimensions of individualism and collectivism, which represents the degree to which a culture emphasizes individual fulfillment and choice versus interdependent relations, social responsibility, and the well–being of the group. Hofstede (2001) characterized "mainstream" culture in the U.S. as the most individualistic of the cultures studied. We will see how various countries rank in terms of their levels of individualism in just a minute. First, we should become more familiar with the characteristics of individualism and collectivism.

With the continuing influx to the U.S. of new students from Mexico and other countries with collectivistic value systems, teachers, counselors, and administrators need an understanding of how and why differing value orientations can cause conflict between home and school. Without this understanding, discord can occur between even the most well–intentioned educators and the students and families they serve. Moreover, internal conflict within the hearts and minds of students may occur when they are pulled between parents (who may desire behaviors consistent with collectivism) and teachers (who stress more individualistic qualities). We saw this in the teacher's quote about home–school conflict.

NOTES

SCRIPT

Overhead 8
Individualism and Collectivism

| Individualism | Collectivism |
|---|---|
| Representative of mainstream U.S. culture | Representative of many immigrant cultures and 70% of the world |
| • Fosters independence and individual achievement | • Fosters interdependence, family, and group success |
| • Emphasizes the physical world, private property, and objects out of context | • Emphasizes the social world, shared property, and objects in social contexts |
| • Promotes individual needs, self-expression, and personal choice | • Promotes norms, respect for authority and elders, and group consensus |

Overhead 8

Move a sheet of paper to uncover each feature comparing individualism and collectivism across each dimension. Note that this slide indicates that 70% of world cultures are collectivistic (Triandis, 1989), and this may confuse participants when they see the relative ranking of countries according to the Hofstede (2001) data. The Triandis data is based upon the percentage of world population in each country whereas the Hofstede data ranks countries or regions from most individualistic to least.

(*Overhead 8*) In this slide, we see three major features of individualism and collectivism. Notice that 70% of world population is collectivistic! No one is exclusively individualistic or collectivistic, but we all have cultural value orientations. When a family from the mainstream culture raises a child in that culture, there is often little conflict between home and school. However, when a family from outside the dominant culture raises a child in the U.S., cultural values can collide. It is important to recognize that both cultural orientations are valid, since all cultures socialize and educate children with purpose.

SCRIPT

(*Overhead 9*) Returning to the research by Hofstede (1980, 1983, 2001), as promised, let's look at the relative value of individualism in a few countries and regions. Notice that the high scores are associated with greater individualism, perhaps indicating an inherent devaluing of the collectivisitic orientation. Where did your family come from? To what degree might they be individualistic or collectivistic? Stop and think about where you stand with your own value system.

NOTES

Overhead 9
Hofstede's Individualism Ratings

| Hofstede's Individualism Ratings | | |
|---|---|---|
| | USA | 91 |
| | Australia | 90 |
| | Great Britain | 89 |
| | Canada | 80 |
| | Italy | 76 |
| | France, Sweden | 71 |
| | Germany | 67 |
| | Israel | 54 |
| | Spain | 51 |
| | India | 48 |
| | Argentina, Japan | 46 |
| | Iran | 41 |
| | "Arab countries," Brazil | 38 |
| | Philippines | 32 |
| | Mexico | 30 |
| | "East African countries" | 27 |
| | Hong Kong | 25 |
| | Singapore, Thailand, "West African countries" | 20 |
| | South Korea | 18 |
| | Costa Rica | 15 |
| | Indonesia, Pakistan | 14 |
| | Guatemala | 6 |

Overhead 9

This overhead shows the relative individualism of some countries and regions. Notice that the highest scores are often in English–speaking and affluent countries. For more information, see Appendix 2, which includes an alphabetical list of fifty countries and three regions and their rankings based on individualism scores from Hofstede's (2001) research. This data is shown to allow presenters and audiences to identify the individualism ranking of their country or region of origin.

## NOTES

Overhead 10
Risk: Overgeneralizing

---

**Risk: Overgeneralizing**

Socioeconomic status, amount of formal education,
and rural or urban origins are powerful predictors of
individualism and collectivism.

All cultures, like people, are both individualistic and
collectivistic and change over time. However, despite
cultural shifts toward the mainstream, child-rearing
values can persist over many generations.

Overhead 10

---

## SCRIPT

While definite cultural differences do exist, and can be understood on the basis of the individualism- collectivism framework, it is necessary to caution you about the limits of the framework and the risks of over–generalizing.

(*Overhead 10*) The framework is not meant to over-simplify groups: Human experience is far too complex to fit into any single scheme. The *Bridging Cultures* framework describes two value systems, not specific people. Socioeconomic status and formal education are powerful predictors of cultural values, much greater than ethnic group membership alone. Many variables comprise family experience, such as if members are from an urban or rural background, whether they had access to formal or only informal education in the country of origin, and the level of their English proficiency. More formal education and higher socioeconomic levels, as well as urban influences, are factors that promote individualism. Less formal education, lower socioeconomic levels, and rural, agricultural lifestyles promote collectivistic culture. Opportunities for formal education, including high school, are often not available to poor people in Mexico, the country of origin of most of the research sample.

All cultures, just like all people, change over time. However, despite cultural shifts toward the mainstream, child–rearing values from the culture of origin may persist over many generations because they come from deeply held beliefs. Social integration with the mainstream may mask the persistence

## SCRIPT

of the ancestral value system, but it often lies just beneath the surface and can exert a strong influence on child rearing (Greenfield & Suzuki, 1998; Lambert, et al., 1979; Valdés, 1996).

(*Overhead 11*) Nevertheless, the value of the *Bridging Cultures* framework (or the continuum of individualism and collectivism) is that it allows people to see one of the major underlying sources of cultural variation. It can be used as a tool to explore cultural differences in a non–judgmental way: Everyone has a culture and no one orientation is right or wrong. It opens the door for inquiry and understanding of others. Do not use the framework to characterize or categorize people but rather to engage them in culturally meaningful personal interactions and to propose solutions to conflict in schools.

We are about to learn more about the framework and its application to education. The following classroom applications are all derived from teacher–initiated and teacher–tested practices prompted by the *Bridging Cultures Project*.

## NOTES

Overhead 11
Benefit: Understanding

**Benefit: Understanding**

The individualism-collectivism framework:

- Provides a tool for uncovering cultural variation
- Opens the door for understanding others
- Helps foster meaningful interactions
- Suggests solutions to conflicts

Overhead 11

If time permits, have participants turn to neighbors and share about the ways in which they might be individualistic and/or collectivistic and how their families tried to raise them, but watch the time!

This is a good place to clarify the framework with an example from your own experience. Participants from collectivistic cultures might especially appreciate your own family story. It is widely acknowledged that examining the values of one's own culture is crucial. Members of the dominant culture may not be used to doing this, and it is often hard for them to make their values explicit for examination. In some cases, my students have lamented that they "don't have a culture!"

This is a good place to ask if there are any questions. Spend a few minutes to clarify misconceptions, but explain that the framework gets clearer once examples are provided in the next part of the presentation.

| NOTES | SCRIPT |
|---|---|

Discussion of the Seven Sources is lengthy, yet participants describe it as especially useful because the examples are vivid and the classroom applications help make individualism and collectivism clear and meaningful. Most important, discussion of the conflicts makes the framework immediately useful.

You may want to take a break during this discussion if the group needs to stretch. If there are time constraints, a condensed version of the Seven Sources is in Handout 2: It can be used with modified explanations.

Overhead 12
Seven Sources of Home-School Conflict

**Seven Sources of Home-School Conflict**

| Individualism | Collectivism |
|---|---|
| · Independence | · Helpfulness |
| · Personal property | · Sharing |
| · Cognitive skills and objects out of context | · Social skills and objects in social context |
| · Child as individual | · Child as part of a family |
| · Parents' role to teach | · Teacher's role to educate |
| · Praise→positive self-esteem | · Criticize→normative behavior |
| · Oral expression | · Listening to authority |

Overhead 12

Uncover one source of conflict at a time. Keep this overhead handy, since you may want to switch between it and the others detailing the seven points. Each source of conflict is accompanied by additional examples and overheads useful to the discussion.

Handout 2
Seven Sources of Home-School Conflict

## Seven Sources of Home–School Conflict
*45 minutes*

The framework of individualism and collectivism has proven to be helpful to teachers in many ways. First, they find that it is not complicated. We often say that the framework is "economical" because it has only two parts to remember and the features of one orientation are understandable in relation to the other. Second, teachers have found that the framework is "generative"; that is, it helps them generate new, almost endless ways to use and apply knowledge of cultural value systems to solve classroom problems and reduce cultural conflict.

(*Overhead 12, Handout 2*) Our discussion now takes us to the Seven Sources of Home–School Conflict (Greenfield, Quiroz, et al., 2000; Quiroz & Greenfield, forthcoming). These are specific areas where the conflicts between individualism and collectivism become real in the lives of teachers, students, and families. In each of the seven topics we will discuss, real–life problems will be described and practical, teacher–generated solutions will be offered. Let's take a look at these sources one by one.

SCRIPT

## Independence versus Helpfulness

Recall that a simple dilemma regarding classroom jobs, such as the one with Salvador and Emanuel, elicited two different views of human development and social relationships. For students, parents, and teachers in School One, the value of independence was prominent. Emanuel had a choice, independent of the needs of others, as to whether he would help a friend or not. This contrasts with the way immigrant Latino parents almost always solved the dilemma: They believed that a student should automatically help a friend in need.

### *Classroom Applications*

Both helpfulness and independence are necessary and important qualities for students. However, classroom culture, as we have seen, often promotes independence at the expense of helpfulness. In fact, helping in academic situations is frequently labeled "cheating" (Rothstein–Fisch, Trumbull, Isaac, Daley, & Pérez, 2001). The *Bridging Cultures* classroom applications therefore often focus on adding collectivistic elements in order to create a better balance between the two value systems. Most important, the goal of *Bridging Cultures* is to make the two value systems of individualism and collectivism explicit to help reduce conflict. Here are some ideas from our *Bridging Cultures* teachers that have made use of this explicit knowledge related to independence and helping.

Questions should be taken at logical intervals throughout the *Module* presentation. The time allotted here can be used to promote additional participant involvement or to synthesize the individualism–collectivism framework with other models of cultural diversity, learning, or teaching.

| NOTES | SCRIPT |
|---|---|

(a) Provide opportunities for students to help as much as possible in order to create classroom harmony. Recognize that helpfulness can have positive educational outcomes for both the helper and the person being helped. When independence is stressed, it can be a single person's independent effort that might contribute to meeting the needs of the whole group.

(b) Assign two monitors for classroom duties so they can help each other, or have the whole class take responsibility of cleaning the entire classroom.

(c) Purposefully allow students to help each other achieve acacdemic success. In one case, a teacher allowed students to seek help from their friends to solve math problems, and the names of the target student and the helper were both written on the answer sheet.

(d) Be explicit about when students can help and when they must work independently, such as in testing situations. Let them know why they will need to work well alone *and* with others.

SCRIPT

NOTES

## Personal property versus Sharing

Return to Overhead 12, Seven Sources. Show the second conflict, Personal property versus Sharing.

(*Overhead 12*) Individualism puts a great deal of emphasis on personal property, while collectivism emphasizes sharing. Objects can be valued more than social relationships in individualistic cultural groups, and social relations are often prized over possessions in collectivistic cultures. Here are two examples.

---

**Seven Sources of Home-School Conflict**

| Individualism | Collectivism |
| --- | --- |
| • Independence | • Helpfulness |
| • Personal property | • Sharing |
| • Cognitive skills and objects out of context | • Social skills and objects in social context |
| • Child as individual | • Child as part of a family |
| • Parents' role to teach | • Teacher's role to educate |
| • Praise→positive self-esteem | • Criticize→normative behavior |
| • Oral expression | • Listening to authority |

Overhead 12

---

### Whose Blocks?

The following example and its interpretation are adapted from Quiroz & Greenfield (forthcoming) and Greenfield, et al. (1996).

Overhead 13
Whose Blocks?

(*Overhead 13*) At preschool, a European American boy was playing with blocks. Nearby, Jasmine, the daughter of immigrant Latino parents, took one of the blocks that the boy was not using and began to play with it. In response, the boy hit Jasmine and she began to cry. The teacher responded by reprimanding the injured, crying Jasmine and admonishing her for taking away toys that belonged to another child!

---

**Whose Blocks?**

Picture this: At preschool, a European American boy was playing with blocks. Nearby, Jasmine, daughter of immigrant Latino parents, took one of the blocks that the boy was not using and began to play with it. In response, the boy hit Jasmine and she began to cry.

What might the teacher think or feel?

What will the teacher do?

Overhead 13

---

It just so happened that Jasmine's mother observed the entire incident from behind a one–way mirror. She became terribly upset that the teacher had failed to reprimand the boy for his act of aggression and instead scolded Jasmine for something that is perceived as completely normal in the family's household, sharing objects. As an immigrant Latina parent, the mother felt that her child was the target of racial discrimination.

*Interpretation*

Jasmine and her mother interpreted the block incident from a collectivistic viewpoint: The boy showed selfishness in refusing to share the toys, and then compounded his undesirable behavior with physical aggression. In contrast, the teacher's reaction was consistent with the individualistic values of independence: Objects are the property of a single individual, if only temporarily (as they are in school). Hence, the teacher treated Jasmine as the primary aggressor because she took away a toy "belonging" to another child.

It is clear that not all teachers from the mainstream U.S. culture would respond as this teacher did. Many would focus on the undesirability of physical aggression or attempt to mediate the dispute in ways that acknowledge the needs of both children. Nevertheless, those with an individualistic orientation, with its valuing of private property, might see the boy as the original victim and Jasmine as an aggressor. In this case, Jasmine was not seen as the victim of the boy's selfishness, and her own legitimate need for rectification went unrecognized.

The values of Jasmine's collectivistic culture were invisible to the teacher, while the underlying values of the teacher were invisible to Jasmine and her mother. This lack of understanding of values resulted in misinterpretations about motives and led to conflict. In this case, Jasmine was confused about the behaviors of both her peer and her teacher, while

SCRIPT

her mother interpreted the attitude of the teacher as an act of discrimination against Latinos.

The default assumption is that the child needs to ask permission to use what is construed in the classroom as "personal property." In order for Jasmine to know that she needs to ask permission, she must understand the assumption that the toys belong to the boy, if only for a period of time, rather than being shared by the group. Jasmine assumed that the blocks were for everyone. This type of cultural misunderstanding can and does lead to conflicts in multicultural classrooms.

Here is another experience related to personal property and sharing.

### Crayons in the Classroom

This case and its analysis are quoted from Quiroz & Greenfield (forthcoming).

(*Overhead 14*) A teacher–mentor came to visit a bilingual kindergarten classroom. The mentor observed that the teacher had arranged the crayons in cups by color—all the red crayons in one cup, all the blue in another, etc.—and that the class was sharing each cup. The mentor suggested putting each child's name on an individual cup that would contain crayons of all colors and would be used by only that particular child.

Overhead 14
Crayons in the Classroom

**Crayons in the Classroom**

A teacher-mentor came to visit a bilingual kindergarten classroom. The mentor observed that the crayons were sorted into cups by color—all the red in one cup, all the blue in another. — and that the class was sharing all the crayons in all the cups.

The mentor suggested putting each child's name on a cup which would contain multicolored crayons which would be used by only that particular child.

Overhead 14

NOTES                                                    SCRIPT

The reason for doing this, the mentor said, was that it was very important for children to have their own property because it made them feel good. She also said that this practice would help children take care of their own property, and that it was only fair that children who took care of their things would not have to use the "crappy" (her word!) material of children who did not know how to take care of their things (Quiroz & Greenfield, forthcoming, p. 12).

*Interpretation*

The crayons incident involves the issue of the underlying value placed on sharing and on personal property. The kindergarten teacher, Blanca Quiroz, is an immigrant Latina parent herself, and her arrangement of the crayons was based on her collectivistic orientation. When she responded to the wishes of the supervising teacher by rearranging the crayons, the children (largely immigrant Latino) found themselves in a conflict between the familiar sharing orientation from home and the emphasis on personal property by the mentor teacher. According to the researchers, the children "did not care if their materials were misplaced, so their 'personal' materials ended up having to be rearranged by the teacher every day. It was not that the children were incapable of arranging their materials in a systematic fashion, because they had done so before. However, the category 'personal material' simply was not important to them" (Quiroz & Greenfield, forthcoming, p. 12).

|  SCRIPT  |  NOTES  |
| --- | --- |

*Classroom Applications*

(a) *(Overhead 15)* School materials may be shared, mutually cared for, and stored where all students have access to them.

Overhead 15
Shared School Supplies

(b) Engage in discussion about when sharing is appropriate and when it might be necessary to "ask permission" before taking something. When squabbles over materials arise, rather than asking, "Who had it first?" have the children find ways to share.

Overhead 15
Shared School Supplies

(c) Families that emphasize sharing often extend this to making gifts to teachers; however, teachers may be uncomfortable accepting presents from families with very limited financial resources. One way for educators to respect the cultural value of sharing is to accept gifts graciously while acknowledging good attendance, a positive attitude, respectfulness, concentrated effort, or helpful behavior.

## NOTES

## SCRIPT

Cognitive skills and objects out of context
 versus Social skills and objects
 in a social context

Return to Overhead 12, Seven Sources, and reveal Cognitive skills versus Social skills.

**Seven Sources of Home-School Conflict**

| Individualism | Collectivism |
|---|---|
| · Independence | · Helpfulness |
| · Personal property | · Sharing |
| · Cognitive skills and objects out of context | · Social skills and objects in social context |
| · Child as individual | · Child as part of a family |
| · Parents' role to teach | · Teacher's role to educate |
| · Praise→positive self-esteem | · Criticize→normative behavior |
| · Oral expression | · Listening to authority |

Overhead 12

*(Overhead 12)* In the individualistic value system, cognitive skills are valued in and of themselves. That is, information about the physical properties of objects is deemed important and worthwhile in its own right. However, collectivistic families see cognitive development as much more embedded in the overall social behavior and manners of children. In collectivistic families, objects are important because they help people. The purpose and benefit of the objects derive from their service to the group.

*How Would You Describe an Egg?*

The next two examples and explanations are from Greenfield, et al., (1996) and Greenfield, Rothstein–Fisch, et al., (2000).

Overhead 16
How Would You Describe an Egg?

**How Would You Describe an Egg?**

A kindergarten teacher showed her class an actual chicken egg that would be hatching soon. She explained the physical properties of the egg and asked the children to describe eggs by thinking about the times they had cooked and eaten eggs.

Overhead 16

*(Overhead 16)* A kindergarten teacher showed her class an actual chicken egg that would be hatching soon. She explained the physical properties of the egg and asked the children to describe eggs by thinking about the times they had cooked and eaten eggs.

One of the children tried three times to talk about how she cooked eggs with her grandmother, but these comments were disregarded in favor of a child who explained that eggs look white and yellow when they are cracked.

SCRIPT

NOTES

## Interpretation

The child's response was typical of the associations encouraged in collectivistic cultures, where objects are most meaningful in connection with social interactions. This teacher expected students to describe eggs as isolated physical entities and did not seem to value the objects as they were used to connect people in social relationships. She was unaware that her question was ambiguous: Children who shared the teacher's value orientation would assume that she was interested in the physical properties of the eggs, although she had not made this point explicit; however, those children who did not share the teacher's value orientation would make a different assumption, that she was interested in the object as a mediator of social relationships.

Ask participants to think about how they would describe eggs based on the times they have cooked and eaten them. Responses typically center on the physical properties of eggs, even when the adult participants are from collectivistic families. Their individualistic responses are likely the result of schooling practices in the U.S.

## Bridging Discourses of Home and School

The "egg incident" and its analysis were included in the initial training of the seven *Bridging Cultures* teachers. A year later, one of the teachers, Marie Altchech, was preparing her fifth–grade class for a field trip to the wetlands. A docent from the area visited her class and asked a series of factual questions, but the students responded with stories of plants and animals experienced with their families. When the docent asked the children to "stop telling stories," their voices fell silent.

The naturalist had beliefs about what counts as knowledge: Scientific knowledge is equated with

NOTES

SCRIPT

knowledge of the physical world and should be discussed independent of social experiences. However, because of her training, the *Bridging Cultures* teacher did not make these same assumptions. After the docent left, she encouraged the children to tell their stories about flora and fauna because she recognized their important role in the implicit assumptions concerning knowledge that her students, children of Latino immigrants, brought to their education. She understood that the stories, which usually connected a natural phenomenon to family members and events, were important in the collectivistic view. She also understood that the docent had quashed her students' voices. This kind of negative experience could stifle students' participation as learners and stunt their confidence (Greenfield, Rothstein–Fisch, et al., 2000). The teacher was not about to let this happen! Instead, she used the students' stories as a foundation to connect the children's lived experiences with the kind of knowledge associated with objects out of context (often referred to as "decontextualized" knowledge). She constructed a chart on the chalkboard showing highlights from the children's stories on the left and scientific information derived from it on the right.

Overhead 17
Science from Stories

**Science from Stories**

| Student experience | Scientific Information |
| --- | --- |
| Carolina's story | Hummingbird qualities |
| • Carolina was playing in the garden with her grandmother | • Brownish with bright iridescent green and red coloring around head and neck |
| • She saw a hummingbird near the cherry tree | • Wings beat rapidly |
| • It "stood in the air" | • Can hover, fly in any direction |
| • Carolina tried to get close to the pretty bird, but it kept moving away | • Must eat frequently because constant energy is required for movements |

Overhead 17

Use a sheet of paper to uncover each section in sequence: Read the left side of the chart first, telling Carolina's story, and then uncover the scientific information in the same sequence the teacher used to construct the chart.

(*Overhead 17*) As we look at this T chart, notice the left side first. The teacher began with giving value to the story as she chronicled some important features of the hummingbird. When Carolina was finished with her story, the teacher guided questions to uncover the scientific elements. Notice that the children learned the word "iridescent," not a typical vocabulary word for fifth graders. Moreover, from the general discussion about hummingbird eating behavior, a larger discourse ensued about metabolic rate. It is doubtful that the docent could ever have promoted such sophisticated vocabulary or scientific awareness by disallowing stories. Clearly, the *Bridging Cultures* teacher valued both the social and scientific information equally—as evidenced by writing almost equal amounts of information on both sides of the chart. The teacher's guided questions based on the child's own story led to uncovering scientific knowledge without the ambiguity seen in the example of the egg.

## Classroom Applications

Rather than denigrating the home culture by discounting important knowledge from the collectivistic frame of reference, the teacher built on the students' knowledge and self–image as competent knowers and learners. The teacher supported the children from collectivistic backgrounds by showing interest in their family experiences and the narrative form, but she was explicit about science and the factual style when that was the topic and mode of study.

(a) Encourage students' stories, appreciating both social and cognitive elements. Value stories in their own right as literature in Spanish, English, or other home language. Use stories as a jumping–off point for lessons in science, social studies, and math.

| NOTES | SCRIPT |
|---|---|

(b) It may be necessary to take only two or three stories when time is limited. Students can also share stories in pairs or small groups.

(c) In conversations with both students and their families, be explicit about questions are that are intended to tap cognitive skills and/or social skills and model how both kinds of knowledge are important and helpful in problem solving.

## Child as an individual versus Child as part of family

Return to Overhead 12, Seven Sources, and reveal Child as an individual versus Child as part of the family.

(*Overhead 12*) Clearly, every child is both an individual and part of a family. However, individualistic families see children as separate individuals. This is strikingly different from collectivistic cultures, where the unit of interest is the family and how any one person contributes to, promotes, or detracts from that whole. How does this play out in school–based policies?

### Seven Sources of Home-School Conflict

| Individualism | Collectivism |
|---|---|
| · Independence | · Helpfulness |
| · Personal property | · Sharing |
| · Cognitive skills and objects out of context | · Social skills and objects in social context |
| · Child as individual | · Child as part of a family |
| · Parents' role to teach | · Teacher's role to educate |
| · Praise→positive self-esteem | · Criticize→normative behavior |
| · Oral expression | · Listening to authority |

Overhead 12

## *School Breakfast and School–Wide Cross–Cultural Misunderstanding*

This real–life experience and explanation come from Quiroz & Greenfield (forthcoming) and Greenfield & Suzuki (1998).

| SCRIPT | NOTES |
|---|---|

---

(*Overhead 18*) There had just been a major crisis in the school involving the federally funded school breakfast program. The problem as seen by the school was that immigrant Latino mothers were accompanying their children to school, bringing younger siblings, and eating the school breakfast together with their children; as a consequence, eating food that "belonged" to only the school children.

When the school tried to stop this practice by locking the families out of the schoolyard, there was a major blow up. Latino immigrant parents who had previously not been involved in school affairs suddenly became activists. The school personnel, who felt strongly about their position, were astounded at the reaction (Quiroz & Greenfield, forthcoming).

*Interpretation*

School officials failed to understand that in the collectivistic worldview of the Latino immigrant parents, it is extremely important for the family to eat together when possible. Instead, administrators and teachers saw this as a transgression against a federal policy which structures the school breakfast program as an individual entitlement, not a family one.

Overhead 18
School Breakfast

**School Breakfast**

There had just been a major crisis involving the federally funded school breakfast program. The problem, as seen by the school, was that immigrant Latina mothers were accompanying their children to school, bringing younger siblings, and eating the school breakfast together with their children; as a consequence, eating food that "belonged" only to the school children.

Overhead 18

<table>
<tr><td>NOTES</td><td>SCRIPT</td></tr>
</table>

Overhead 19
School Sign

Ask participants if they have seen similar signs or to reflect on how they might feel as the parents in this case.

(*Overhead 19*) Consider this photo, "Only students are permitted in eating area." What's the message? "Stay out!" Although the sign is translated into Spanish, there is no explanation of why this rule exists. Stop and think for a moment how very strange this message might be to collectivistic families where eating together is among the most basic elements in life. Incidentally, this was the only sign at the school; there weren't any that said, "Welcome families" or "We're glad you're here!"

As a result of learning about the school breakfast problem in a *Bridging Cultures* training workshop, one of the teachers, Catherine Daley, became proactive in her school. Ms. Daley's school had to enforce a new "locked school" policy, in which gates and access points to the outside would be locked during the day. The teacher knew that parents would feel unwelcome in the closed school. She discussed the policies and how they might be interpreted from a collectivistic perspective with a school administrator, which resulted in sending a letter to families in English and Spanish explaining the reasons behind the policies about federally subsidized food and children's safety at school.

Overhead 20
School Letter

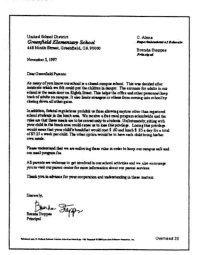

(*Overhead 20*) Here is the English version of the letter that was sent out. It does a fine job of highlighting school policy by explaining the underlying reasons for the rules explicitly. It also welcomes parent involvement. In addition to sending a letter, explaining the policy face–to–face with the families is important since parents may have limited literacy

SCRIPT                                                     NOTES

skills and may not read Spanish or English or may
be fearful of something on official letterhead. Ideally,
a school–wide family information network could
help convey school policies and promote understanding of home and school practices.

This example illustrates that teachers *and* administrators need to be aware of how their messages may
be perceived from a different cultural vantage point
and cultivate ways to share understanding. In a
similar case, a catastrophe between staff and parents was averted because *Bridging Cultures* teacher
Giancarlo Mercado recognized the problem of a
locked–down, closed campus from Ms. Daley's experience. At his principal's request, he held meetings for school staff making the cultural values of
many immigrant families explicit for all concerned
(Rothstein–Fisch, 2000). No crisis ensued, and the
staff seemed to recognize the value of understanding the cultural framework of individualism and
collectivism.

## NOTES

## SCRIPT

Here is another example of misunderstanding.

*The Parent–Teacher Conference*

This example and discussion are quoted from a videotaped study of nine naturally occurring conferences between immigrant Latino parents and their child's European American teacher (Greenfield, Quiroz, & Raeff, 2000).

This is a good place to discuss the article from the *Readings* (Article 3) on parent–teacher conferences (Quiroz, et al., 1999). Several of my graduate students who are elementary school teachers have had great success with group parent–teacher conferences. They organized the conferences around reading levels, and the parents seemed relieved to learn that other families had the same questions or concerns. The teachers reported that the parents, who generally said little on a one–to–one basis, became vocal in a group context. Teachers also felt less frustration because they could spend more time with families as a group explaining state standards, report cards, and other generic information, rather than repeating the same explanations over and over again in individual 20–minute conferences. As an incidental by–product of the group conferences, the families offered parenting advice to each other in a manner that was more akin to what they had experienced in their country of origin.

In one video, the teacher began with this statement to the father: "She's doing great, she's doing beautifully in English and in reading. And in writing, and in speaking." The father showed discomfort, looking down at his lap, and turned the conversation toward his son (present at the conference), saying "the same [with] this guy. . ." only to be interrupted by the teacher's shrill voice (indicating *her* discomfort with the changed focus of the meeting). As she maneuvered the conference conversation back to the daughter, the child in her class, the father stopped responding to her comments (Greenfield, Quiroz, et al., 2000, p. 100).

The excerpt from the parent–teacher conference provides a good example of cross–cultural miscommunication. Neither the teacher nor the father did or said what the other wanted or expected. The father did not follow up on the teacher's lead and discuss the academic excellence of his daughter as an individual; likewise, the teacher did not seem to be aware that the father's orientation was toward the academic merits of the family as a unit. In other words, he was oriented to the family as a unit, rather than the singling out of only one child.

### Interpretation

The discord between the two adults results from differing cultural value systems. The parent's collectivistic orientation—maintaining the family as a unit—was in conflict with the teacher's individualistic orientation—singling out this particular student. The negative impact on home–school relations was intensified because neither participant recognized that there was a communication problem during the conversation; thus there was no attempt to address the basic misunderstanding (Greenfield, Quiroz, & Raeff, 2000).

In both the school breakfast crisis and the parent–teacher conference miscommunication, the parents were trying to keep the family together as a unit. This conflicts directly with implicit school values and with explicit school policies that focus on the child as an individual.

### Classroom Applications

(a) Teachers should find out what the family's beliefs and goals are so that students' success in school does not inadvertently violate the family's cultural conceptions of success. Sharing information about school expectations and norms helps ensure that parents understand the U.S. educational system and its culture, but we must also listen to and learn from families. With the

| NOTES | SCRIPT |
|---|---|
| | help of an interpreter if need be, describe the philosophical underpinnings of the U.S., which was founded on rights of the individual. In some cases, it is not always possible or reasonable to achieve individualism and family success, such as when a child is kept out of school to help a sick relative, but creative flexibility can make a difference. For example, sending a homework packet to the absent child while she or he cares for a relative can help minimize academic peril. |

(b) Promote family empowerment in school practices and policies through parent–led meetings that welcome children and other family members to convey openness and address concerns. Potluck gatherings are especially helpful in attracting families, setting a positive tone, and showing the commitment of teachers who sincerely want to work with families to support student success. Inviting parents to bring food is also likely to resonate with the home value of helping and sharing.

(c) Group parent conferences have been successful in providing a voice for parents who may be more comfortable discussing children as a group rather than singling out individuals. (See also *Readings*, Article 3.)

SCRIPT                                                    NOTES

Parents' role to teach versus
Teacher's role to educate

Parents' role versus teacher's role is the next conflict.

(*Overhead 12*) The educational maxim that parents
are their children's first teachers guides the thinking
of many educators (National Education Goals Panel,
2000). Schools often send letters home urging parents to work in specific ways with their children,
such as practicing reading, editing homework, or
completing math assignments.

(*Overhead 21*) Valdés (1966) found that all 10 of
the immigrant Latina mothers she studied "saw themselves as participating actively in their children's
*educación*; that is, in raising children to be good and
well–behaved human beings. They did not, however,
see themselves as adjunct schoolteachers. They did
not see their role as involving the teaching of school
subjects. In their own experience in school, this had
been the province of the teacher. Mothers, on the
other hand, had been responsible for the moral upbringing of their children. When American teachers expected that Mexican working–class mothers
would 'help' their children with their schoolwork,
they were making assumptions about the abilities
that the mothers did not have. Moreover, they were
also making assumptions about the universality of
what, in American schools, counts as knowledge"
(p. 166).

It may be unrealistic to expect that parents will take
on didactic roles with their children (Quiroz &

Return to Overhead 12, Seven Sources,
and show Parents' role versus Teacher's
role.

**Seven Sources of Home-School Conflict**

| Individualism | Collectivism |
|---|---|
| · Independence | · Helpfulness |
| · Personal property | · Sharing |
| · Cognitive skills and objects out of context | · Social skills and objects in social context |
| · Child as individual | · Child as part of a family |
| · Parents' role to teach | · Teacher's role to educate |
| · Praise→positive self-esteem | · Criticize→normative behavior |
| · Oral expression | · Listening to authority |

Overhead 12

Overhead 21
Parents' Role versus Teacher's Role

**Parents' Role versus Teacher's Role**

In a study of immigrant Latino families, Valdés found
that mothers "saw themselves as participating actively
in their children's *educación*, that is, in raising children
to be good and well-behaved human beings. They did
not, however, see themselves as adjunct schoolteachers.
They did not see their role as involving the teaching of
school subjects. In their own experience in school, this
had been the province of the teacher."

Overhead 21

Put up Overhead 21 but display only the title
initially. Then uncover the quote.

NOTES

SCRIPT

Greenfield, forthcoming). For example, many immigrant Latino come to the U.S. with six or fewer years of formal education. Moreover, the educational system of the country of origin is quite different from that of the U.S. (Trumbull, Rothstein–Fisch, et al., 2001). Even more important, these parents want the schools to allow them to teach what they consider proper social behavior and values to their children without obstructing the socialization process. Nevertheless, many times parent education does interfere—by expecting parents to teach their children in individualistic ways (Greenfield, Quiroz, & Raeff, 2000; Trumbull, Rothstein–Fisch, et al., 2001; Valdés, 1996).

*Teachers Giving Parenting Advice*

Another finding of the previously mentioned conferences between immigrant Latino parents and their children's European American elementary school teachers was that in seven of the nine cases, parents were uncooperative when the teacher tried to offer parenting advice. The parents seemed to believe that, at home, parenting was up to them. In addition, the parents may have been particularly suspicious of the teachers' suggestions, fearing that the teachers' "ideal" child would be learning behaviors inconsistent with the home values of collectivism. Thus, taking the advice of the teacher might undermine the parents' goals for helping, sharing, and behaviors related to other collectivistic values (Greenfield, Quiroz, & Raeff, 2000).

SCRIPT                                                    NOTES

*Classroom Applications*

(a) Often the first question immigrant Latino parents ask teachers is, "*¿Como se porta mi hijo/ hija?*" "How is my child behaving?" The parents may see a distinct role for teachers as responsible for teaching reading, writing, and math; however, they see themselves as responsible for moral education. Explicitly recognize when parents have well–behaved children.

(b) (*Overhead 22*) Be realistic about expectations regarding homework. It might be helpful to ask which family members, such as older siblings or cousins, can help students with homework. One *Bridging Cultures* teacher avoids conflicts by allowing students to practice homework in small groups without writing down the answers. Students practice homework as a group, reviewing their lessons and discussing appropriate responses so they can complete it at home on their own. As a result, the homework completion rate increased to 100%.

Overhead 22
Group Homework Practice

(c) Rethink student–led conferences. Their format turns out to be incompatible with collectivistic values. Putting the child in charge of a conference violates a parent's expectation of being respected and according the teacher proper authority. Instead, try group conferences with the option to follow up with an individual conference if desired.

(d) Ensure that schools are welcoming to parents with limited formal education. Invite them to come and learn more about educational goals and

| NOTES | SCRIPT |
|---|---|

processes just as you listen to matters of family concern. Parent centers located at school sites (and often run by immigrant parents themselves) can increase meaningful communication about schools and create a social hub for family support (Joint Committee to Develop a Master Plan for Education, 2002; Moles, 1996).

## Praise versus Criticism

The sixth source of home-school conflict is the tension between praise and criticism.

(*Overhead 12, Overhead 23*) A Mexican immigrant mother recalls her experience in a parent–teacher conference in which her child's teacher called her daughter "outstanding." According to this mother, "I did not know what to do about her being 'outstanding': I had tried to show my daughter not to 'show off' or be cruel to others, but it seemed that it was not working. I blamed her 'bad habit' of 'standing out' on this country's social influences as I had seen on TV and in my personal observations" (Quiroz & Greenfield, forthcoming, p. 6).

Parents with a strong collectivistic orientation are likely to become uncomfortable when they hear praise of their children. Praise singles a child out from a group. Consider the literal meaning of "outstanding"—standing out from the group. Collectivistic parents may not consider this a positive trait. On the contrary, it may be cause for concern! Indi-

---

**NOTES column:**

Return to Overhead 12, Seven Sources, and reveal Praise versus criticism.

**Seven Sources of Home-School Conflict**

| Individualism | Collectivism |
|---|---|
| · Independence | · Helpfulness |
| · Personal property | · Sharing |
| · Cognitive skills and objects out of context | · Social skills and objects in social context |
| · Child as individual | · Child as part of a family |
| · Parents' role to teach | · Teacher's role to educate |
| · Praise→positive self-esteem | · Criticize→normative behavior |
| · Oral expression | · Listening to authority |

Overhead 12

Overhead 23
Praise versus Criticism

**Praise versus Criticism**

A Mexican immigrant mother recalls her experience in a parent-teacher conference in which her child's teacher called her daughter "outstanding." According to this mother, "I did not know what to do about her being 'outstanding': I had tried to show my daughter not to 'show off' or be cruel to others, but it seemed it was not working. I blamed her 'bad habit' of 'standing out' on this country's social influences as I had seen on TV and in my personal observations."

Overhead 23

SCRIPT

vidualistic systems highlight the value of praise to maintain positive self–esteem. In collectivistic systems, criticism is valued as a feedback mechanism that encourages normative behavior. Collectivistic students may become very uncomfortable when they hear teachers reitreate, "You're great," "You're the best!" Notice the strong emphasis on self and on being better than others in these expressions. Latino immigrant parents may fear that praise will make children egotistical.

## The Concept of "Burro"

Some teachers report hearing parents call their child a "burro"—literally translated as "donkey." They interpret this as a demeaning self–fulfilling prophecy that will cause children to develop negative self–esteem. However, within the home culture, using such nicknames is an important way to remind children to focus attention on schoolwork or the task at hand. The criticism is meant to foster normative behavior so that individuals do not become isolated from their group. Moreover, Latino immigrant parents may assume that students do not have to be praised for expected behaviors that should come naturally to them.

## Mocking the Praise

In two different instances, collectivistic students subjected to praise appeared to scoff at the acclaim. In one case, a quiet student was being tutored in long division. Because she appeared shy, the tutor

## NOTES

There is obvious overlap among many of the examples of the Seven Points of Conflict. This is natural since all the examples pivot on the elements of individualism and collectivism. For example, elements from "Praise versus Criticism" link to the differences between parents' and teacher's roles.

## SCRIPT

believed she lacked self–confidence and praised her repeatedly for the smallest efforts, saying, "Good" or "That's right, nice work!" As the student began to work the math problems, she was overhead muttering sarcastically under her breath, "Nice work." In another case, a college student was tutoring a group of immigrant high school girls in English. He constantly used praise in a manner that he felt would be motivating to the young women. However, on the bus ride home from school, the girls mocked his praise and imitated his comments chorally in a sing–song manner; "Good job," they mimicked and then erupted in giggles (Geary, 2001).

In both cases, the tutors' attempts at positive motivation actually had the reverse effect: The collectivistic students were not motivated by the praise; instead they made fun of it. These students were from a culture in which they were used to criticism, not praise, as motivation. Immigrant children are not the only ones who may suffer from excessive or insincere praise. Kohn (1993) denounces "phony praise" (p. 109) and questions the value of praise that sets up competition. He also condemns public praise as undermining intrinsic motivation.

### Rethinking Academic Award Activities

Equipped with the framework, a colleague of a *Bridging Cultures* teacher began to recognize the underlying cause of her students' resistance to the monthly Awards Assembly. She had never understood why her kindergarten children would ask repeatedly if they could stay in their class and not attend the ceremony that highlighted "best attendance," "best reader," and, apparently worst of all, "most improved." The teacher hypothesized as a result of learning the framework of individualism and collectivism that the children resisted the idea of the praise: It isolated them from the group, and both they and their schoolmates felt uncomfortable about that. The children wanted to avoid the praise! This recognition sparked a novel idea. The teacher, supported by her principal, was allowed to teach her whole class a dance (with valuable music, rhythm, and movement benefits for all) to be performed during the regular assembly. The children were proud to entertain the other students and seemed to feel far more accomplished than when they were pulled away for individual praise in isolation from the group.

## Classroom Applications

(a) Use praise parsimoniously, authentically, and specifically to promote learning. Less is more in the case of praise. Teacher comments such as "I like the way you helped Luis" seem especially vacant since "helping" is likely to be something the student would do automatically. Statements that give information about performance, such as "clever idea," "good examples," or "well punctuated," are much more helpful than undifferentiated praise.

(b) Private praise may honor the student more than public praise. Focus public praise on whole–class achievements such as when the whole class attains a language arts, math, or science goal.

NOTES

SCRIPT

(c) Expressing authentic disappointment may be an honest way to motivate students. Explaining errors is an important feedback mechanism, and it may be more consistent with home culture. Refrain from either praise or criticism by asking students, "Is this your best work?" to promote their own internal motivation and self–knowledge.

(d) Rethink awards assemblies as merely show-casing selected individuals and instead find a way to emphasize the success of the group such as learning a dance, mastering a certain level of timed math facts, or raising the attendance rate at school.

Oral expression
versus Listening to authority

The last conflict we will discuss is oral expression versus listening to authority.

Return to Overhead 12, Seven Sources, and reveal Oral expression versus Listening to authority.

(*Overhead 12*) Skilled self–expression, critical questioning, and the ability to engage in debate are often assumed to be valued attributes of the "ideal student." With this in mind, individualistic parents may prepare their children for school by socializing them to "speak up," "ask a lot of questions," or "tell the teacher if you need anything." This would be very consistent with a "constructivist" theory of learning that emphasizes a child's active participation in making meaning (Trumbull, et al., 2000).

| **Seven Sources of Home-School Conflict** | |
|---|---|
| **Individualism** | **Collectivism** |
| · Independence | · Helpfulness |
| · Personal property | · Sharing |
| · Cognitive skills and objects out of context | · Social skills and objects in social context |
| · Child as individual | · Child as part of a family |
| · Parents' role to teach | · Teacher's role to educate |
| · Praise→positive self-esteem | · Criticize→normative behavior |
| · Oral expression | · Listening to authority |

Overhead 12

SCRIPT

NOTES

However, children from collectivistic cultures are socialized very differently. They are taught to listen respectfully to authority figures and to learn by watching others. Rather than telling the teacher if they need anything, they are instructed by parents not to bother the teacher with their own needs because that would take time away from the lesson. Their individual questions would also pull them away from being part of the whole group, causing conflict comparable to what we have seen in other examples.

(*Overhead 24*) Teachers often attribute reluctance to participate in class discussions to quietness, limited English proficiency, or shyness. These perceptions miss the underlying role of culture in oral expression. In individualistic cultures, it is often said, "The squeaky wheel gets the grease." However, the axiom in collectivistic cultures is, "The nail that sticks up gets pounded down."

*Checking for Understanding*

One *Bridging Cultures* teacher, Elvia Hernandez, whose class is a combination kindergarten and first and second grades, noted that the children rarely raised their hands to ask questions. This continued to be true of students in her class for one or two years. "When I asked if they understand something, the children always nodded affirmatively. By that I mean, if I am teaching a lesson, they won't say, 'I don't understand.' But in small groups, then I will re-explain the concept because I will think about

Facilitators are encouraged to link the question of oral expression versus listening to authority to examples of power–distance and verbal versus non–verbal communication styles. For instance, the individualistic value orientation tends to be associated with more direct, low–context forms of communication. Similarly, in the U.S., individualism is also associated with low power–distance, which assumes shared responsibility between teachers, students, and parents for the educational process. (See Brislin & Yoshida, 1994; Guerra & Garcia, 2000; and Lustig & Koester, 1999.)

Comparing oral expression to listening can prompt an important discussion of communication in general. Invite participants to share examples of this conflict from their personal experiences. Although this definitely adds more time to the presentation, it is a valuable strategy to engage the audience personally and meaningfully.

Overhead 24
Oral expression versus
Respect for authority.

**Oral Expression versus
Respect for Authority**

In individualistic cultures, it is often said
that "the squeaky wheel gets the grease."

In collectivistic cultures, it's often said that
"the nail that sticks up gets pounded down"!

Overhead 24

## NOTES

## SCRIPT

the [*Bridging Cultures*] model—from what we learned, they are not the type to question authority or they don't want to be highlighted or stand out in the group. So I pull them aside once everyone else is working and I just give them an extra problem or explanation without asking them, 'What don't you understand?' Somehow I will indirectly give them more when I know they didn't understand a concept. You can see how they breathe better, then I can send them along and they can do their work" (Rothstein–Fisch, 2000).

### Guilt in the Principal's Office

Overhead 25
Guilt in the Principal's Office

(*Overhead 25*) A child from a Mexican American family was called into the principal's office, accused of a school–related crime. The child, out of respect, did not look at the principal during the questioning. The principal incorrectly assumed this behavior represented shame. The child was assumed to be guilty and was expelled. As it turned out, another child who was also questioned was guilty of the crime, but because he looked directly at the principal and spoke up, he was assumed to be innocent. *Bridging Cultures* teacher, Catherine Daley, decided to make "looking into eyes" an explicit lesson for her students. She had a discussion with her third grade class about eye contact. The children were clearly told that different people and different situations required different kinds of looking. She told them, "If you are with a Latino, look down, and when you are with a typical American you must look them in the eyes." Ms. Daley wanted to be very clear that culture affects how different people interpret the same behavior. Following the discussion, she took the children on a "field trip" around the school to identify which school adults they should lower their eyes for and which they should look at eye–to–eye. In addition, she cautioned the students not to overgeneralize or make too many assumptions by telling them, "If the other person is not getting the right message, try switching the eye contact level." (Rothstein–Fisch, 2000.)

These two examples illustrate the importance of demystifying cultural differences to bridge the gap between behavior that demonstrates respect at home (looking down and being a respectful listener) and behavior that shows respect at school (looking at the person speaking and asking questions). As in the other sources of home–school conflict, it is essential for students to learn both sets of skills. They need to know how to show respect for authority and what is considered appropriate oral expression in school.

### Classroom Applications

(a) Be explicit about when it is appropriate for students to ask questions and when it is appropriate to listen. Let them ask each other questions in pairs or small groups where age and authority differences will not inhibit oral expression. Provide opportunities for students to role–play signs of respect for different people or write stories about cultural misunderstandings.

| NOTES | SCRIPT |
|---|---|
| | (b) Don't assume that quiet children are not learning or that they are shy. Understand that just because they are not speaking does not mean they are not comprehending and learning. Watch children in the yard or in other peer situations to see their verbal skills at work. To evaluate language, observe them in small groups or pairs as they complete academic tasks. Evaluate proficiency through both individual and group discussion or through other formal measures both oral and written.<br><br>(c) Allow students to present oral work in groups so that even when they are the only person talking, they are part of their group at the front of the class thus alleviating their stress in speaking out alone. |

| SCRIPT | NOTES |
|---|---|

## You Are the Bridge
*15 minutes*

(*Overhead 26*) While *Bridging Cultures* may seem to emphasize differences between individualism and collectivism, the foremost idea of the *Project* is actually about making bridges *between* cultures. Both individualism and collectivism have their benefits and disadvantages, and a person may be more individualistic or collectivistic in different situations, depending on the people in those settings. The goals of this workshop are to make the invisible cultural differences discernible and to suggest teacher–constructed learning experiences that truly bridge cultures.

Overhead 26
You are the Bridge

**You Are the Bridge**

Envision that you are building a cultural bridge.

1. What does the bridge connect?

2. How long and wide would it be?

3. What materials would be used to construct the bridge and who would build it?

4. What would the bridge look like?

Draw the bridge.

Overhead 26

| NOTES | SCRIPT |
|---|---|

### Bridge Activity

Handout 3
You are the Bridge

To help educators focus on what they can do to bridge cultures, an activity to help visualize the symbolic bridge between individualism and collectivism is offered. Participants report that this activity has been enormously valuable for several reasons:

· It allows them to get in touch with their own cultural experiences in a visual manner

· It provides a situated reality of others' experiences

· It lingers as a potent image for educators when they are confronted with home–school conflict

Distribute Handout 3 or blank paper. Sharing can be done in groups of five or fewer followed by a short debriefing with specific examples and insights. If the group is not too large, invite as many as wish to share and describe bridges.

Examples have included:

· A toll bridge which exacts a heavy price when a person tries to be bicultural

· A frightening suspension bridge, wobbly and faltering, causing great fear and trepidation

· A brick bridge so wide that many people can cross it arm–in–arm and in sync. It has benches and footlights. It can be a resting place or a place to see things in a new way that could not be predicted by those on only the individualistic side or the collectivistic side.

(*Handout 3*) Now it is your turn to construct a cultural bridge. In this activity, you will use your imagination and creativity. Pause for a moment and close your eyes. Slow your breathing and clear your mind. How would you build a cultural bridge? Spend a moment to envision your cultural bridge.

1. What does the bridge connect?

2. How long and wide would it be?

3. What materials would be used to construct the bridge and who would build it?

4. What would the bridge look like? Now, draw the bridge you see!

Who would like to share their bridge?

Questions from the audience (as time permits).

| SCRIPT | NOTES |
|---|---|

## Evaluation
*10 minutes*

(*Handout 4*) It is time to complete a written evaluation to help you integrate your learning while providing important feedback for the instructor. Please provide as much information as possible on the evaluation form.

Handout 4
*Bridging Cultures* between
Home and School Evaluation

Distribute handout. This is a prototype of an evaluation and, as mentioned earlier, you are encouraged to create your own, addressing your unique questions and concerns. The merits of evaluation data are discussed in the next section.

# Chapter **3**

## Effect of the *Module* on Pre–Service Teachers

What kind of impact can a teacher–educator expect to have on teachers in a matter of three hours (plus a little follow–up, if one is fortunate enough to find the time)? I was very interested in answering this question as I began to integrate the *Bridging Cultures* framework into my education courses at California State University, Northridge. This chapter describes my attempt to answer this question. In 1997, I presented a version of this *Module* to my college students, all of whom were teachers–in–training. Since that initial field test of the *Module*, many refinements and improvements have been made. Nevertheless, the data I collected on three occasions during that semester contain the "voice" of the students as they learned about the framework of individualism and collectivism and reflected on it during the semester. The students' voice is presented in this chapter because it provides a glimpse of what can be accomplished in a single three–hour course period. Before presenting the outcomes, the context of the course, students, and instruction is described.

## The Course

All students were enrolled in a course titled "Psychological Foundations K–12," designed to provide "an overview of the theoretical positions on learning, development, and instruction which attempt to shape the outcome of elementary and secondary education" (California State University Catalog, 1996–1998, p. 243). The course is offered as an upper division undergraduate requirement for students seeking a teaching credential at either the elementary or secondary level. In the fall of 1997, I offered two sections of the course. Each section met for three hours (4:00 p.m.–7 :00 p.m.) one day a week for 15 weeks. The course included topics such as theories of development and learning, motivation, classroom planning and management, and assessment.

## The Students

About two–thirds of the students were under-graduates and the other third were graduate students. Approximately one–third were already working in classrooms as emergency–credential teachers or substitute teachers; about two–thirds had not had previous teaching experience. However, all students were required to complete 15 hours of classroom observation and participation as part of the course so that everyone had direct experience with elementary or secondary students who might come from diverse cultural backgrounds. The ethnic identification of the students was not available several years after the evaluations were conducted. I recall that they were about 70% European American, 20% Latino, and 10% African American, Asian Pacific Islander, or from other ethnic or cultural backgrounds. (At the time I pilot–tested the *Module* in 1997, I could not have imagined the impact it was going to have, and thus, I did not collect background information on my student–participants.) Student age ranged from early twenties to early fifties. One course was taught on the main campus of CSUN (n = 25, 20 women, 5 men) and the other at the satellite campus in Ventura, California (n = 29, all women). Some students did not participate in all three evaluations described in this chapter due to absences on a given day.

## The Instructor

During the semester the course was offered, I had been a staff researcher on the *Bridging Cultures Project* for the two years of its existence. Using the individualism and collectivism framework as a basis for longitudinal teacher professional development had an impressive impact on in–service teachers. Therefore, I was curious about its usefulness for teachers–in–training. At the time, I had been teaching at CSUN for over 10 years, but this was the first semester I taught the Psychological Foundations, K–12 course.

## Procedure

In the second month of the semester, students were told that the class session would focus on a framework for understanding cross–cultural values in school. The *Bridging Cultures Project* was introduced as a collaboration among researchers at WestEd (a regional educational laboratory), the UCLA Department of Psychology, CSUN, and seven bilingual teachers from elementary schools in the greater Los Angeles area. The *Module* was presented in the same format to each class during the same week of the semester. Each presentation lasted slightly less than three hours, allowing time for academic housekeeping prior to presenting the *Module* and break time.

## *Bridging Cultures Module* Assessment Results

The impact of the *Module* was assessed on three separate occasions. First, credential students were asked to evaluate *Bridging Cultures* immediately after the presentation. The second evaluation occurred three weeks later as part of a midterm examination in which students were asked to "describe the five most salient parts of the *Bridging Cultures* model." The third evaluation consisted of a total course review in the context of a final exam. To prepare for the final exam, students were instructed to think back over the whole semester and prepare a response to the following: "Describe the five most valuable things you learned in the course and cite how each might be applied in your own classroom."

The data derived from each of these three evaluations is included in this chapter because it tends to validate the content and process suggested in the *Module*. However, without pretests or baseline information, it is impossible to gauge how many students may have entered the course with prior knowledge of the concepts of individualism and collectivism. Furthermore, I have no way of knowing if there were differences between the elementary and secondary education majors. Although most of the examples in the *Module* have come from elementary schools, my experience in using the *Module* since 1997 has shown that the examples translate reasonably well to teachers–in–training of early childhood and secondary students, as well as school counselors–in–training. In general, participants seemed adept at connecting the framework to their own lived experiences, fieldwork placements, and worksites. Nevertheless, the following results do not tell us anything about the long–term effects of the *Module* after the semester of training, and we have no way of knowing if the initial enthusiasm for the *Bridging Cultures Project* has been translated into practice.

Can other professors or professional development specialists expect the same level of success presented here? As a staff researcher, I was deeply immersed in the framework and knew the material very well. As a result of classroom observations and interviews with each *Bridging Cultures* teacher, I had firsthand knowledge of how the framework worked in practice and my students knew I was enthusiastic about the *Project*. Clearly, the evaluation data presented are influenced by my knowledge and passion for cultural diversity.

However, the data also represent my very first presentation of the *Module*, and so in that sense they represent the experiences of a novice presenter. In the time since the original *Module* was drafted, pilot–tested, and evaluated, it has become more sophisticated and fine–tuned. Although the data reported in this chapter may have benefited from my zeal, peers who have used the *Module* have reported similar positive outcomes. Moreover, when I first presented it, I was a relative newcomer to the field of multicultural education. Educators with prior experience, study, or training in cross–cultural or multicultural education would be more adept at integrating the *Module* into other diversity training material.

## Evaluation 1
## Exit Evaluation of
## the *Bridging Cultures Module*

At the end of each of the two *Bridging Cultures* classroom presentations, education students were asked to evaluate the experience. Both the content and the method of the presentation were assessed. Overall, students were very positive (n = 46 of 47 respondents). The results of the open–ended questions revealed five major themes:

- A new awareness of cultural influences on education

- The relevance of the framework to teachers and their students, families, and schools

- The economical value of the framework, which organizes interrelated ideas into a two part system

- A sense of generativity—thinking beyond the immediate applications offered in the class to new ways of solving classroom problems

- Personal meaning that could be applied to cultural beliefs about self, family, and friends as well as students and schools

The complete set of responses to the questions, "What is the relevancy of the model for you?" and "How can you apply the model to yourself and your work?" is offered in the next section. The responses are organized around the five themes identified above, along with a brief narrative introduction of each theme. Students' comments are just as they crafted them. They are all marked as "Written Comments."

## New Awareness and Understanding

Becoming aware that all people have cultures and that no one culture is inherently better than another is the first goal of the *Module*. Before educators can work effectively with students and families from diverse cultures, they must become aware of their own culture. Yet this can be problematic for students (typically European American), who sometimes report that they don't have a culture! Once educators understand that everyone has a culture, they can begin to appreciate the culture of others as well as recognize the nuances of school culture. In addition, awareness is an important first step in reducing cultural conflict (Brislin & Yoshida, 1994; Guerra & Garcia, 2000). Did students gain a new awareness of cultures as a result of the *Bridging Cultures* presentation? Did the framework of individualism and collectivism promote new understanding?

### Written Comments

What interested me most about the lecture was the notion that most of us have preconceived ideas regarding the way we think people want to be taught/treated. For example, I was surprised that the Latino culture does not value being "*outstanding*". I assumed that every parent would love to hear a teacher exclaim how their child stands above the rest. After learning how [different] cultures value helpfulness and collectivism rather than competition and individualism, I have acquired a heightened respect for their culture.

It is a new concept for me in relation to contact with other cultures. It helped me to take one more step beneath the surface of relating to others. It will help me understand or at least be open to bridging rather than judging.

There is a lot to learn about the thinking process of other cultures. [I have] awareness of potential for misunderstanding and the value of other cultures perspectives.

We need to be aware of this in order to help our students and enrich their lives. Good examples. Opened my eyes.

I am better aware of cultural differences. I was not aware that teachers could offend by promoting individualism. In the future, I may be faced with other cultures and word choice will be important. The examples bring in the relevance.

Having an understanding of this model will help give me insight so I can be more emphatic [empathic] to people's differences.

It makes me aware of how students come to school with different attitudes and expectations. I can appreciate the differences among people.

[It] Leads to a greater understanding of the different perspectives I should be looking at in my classroom.

It made my understanding more clear. It's a topic that generally comes up in social conversations with my friends and husband. Some of it holds true to my own personal philosophies.

Good at giving personal awareness and understanding where students are coming from.

Well I think it is very eye–opening to understand the differences and I will be excited to see how both are used and if [they are] in harmony.

To serve our students better with both priorities [we] should be aware and open to differences and try to find some mid–ground where both parties are content.

When I become a teacher, I will try to understand the population of children and their culture. On a personal note, we are a collective family. On an educational note: it gives me a greater understanding into the conflict of parent and school.

I have gained a fuller understanding of where students are coming from.

Even though I've been exposed to these cultures, it is from the outside in. I feel like I got a clear view from the inside.

By understanding the differences, I will try to bridge the gap between the two. It was very informative, interesting and wonderful. I'm glad that I've learned a lot from this presentation.

It put some of my past experiences into perspective. This model will allow me to be more aware and recognize some cultural differences.

## Relevance

Did the *Module* provide a framework that teacher–credential students could find applicable to their future careers with students and families? Students cited the usefulness of the examples to working with parents as being particularly relevant.

### Written Comments

I can relate the model to my classroom experience——to understand my students and work on communication. Almost all of my students are Latin[o] immigrants. I will remind myself daily (almost daily) that my students have a different background . . . and are motivated by different things.

[The model] relates directly to how one interacts not just in the classroom but everywhere with people who practice collectivism. I will listen to the parents based on what I have learned about collectivism and will present information differently.

Information is relevant only when I can take it back to the classroom——which I could with this information. In talking with Hispanic parents I can be more aware of why they may react the way they do.

This would be so useful for teachers to be educated on this so we can apply it in our classrooms. We are constantly being informed on how cultural differences affect student learning. This module gave me actual ways of handling these differences.

The model of individualism and collectivism is of great interest to me because I am sure when I am hired as a teacher I will come into contact with similar experiences. This offers me a new perspective. The striking examples mentioned in class offered a clear view of the different developmental scripts.

The concrete examples and the historical background [contributed to the success of the *Module*].

It was helpful, [it is] important to have this knowledge when dealing with parents and to learn more about different cultures.

I have heard of this before but it was nice to be refreshed. I need to be aware of different cultural patterns and to match my communication (verbal and non–verbal).

When I teach, I will integrate it.

## Economy

We like to say that the framework of individualism and collectivism is economical because it integrates many seemingly separate elements into a two–part system. Although our goal has never been to oversimplify, the framework does consolidate several elements of cultural variation and thus it provides an efficient way of thinking about the possibilities of cultural value differences. Did teachers–in–training gravitate to the economy of a two part framework?

### Written Comments

There are so many different theories mentioned in various courses, but to be given enough information and examples of one really makes it approachable, interesting, and sparks a want for more. I will consider these when working with children and when evaluating parent involvement and interaction as well as in relations with co-workers.

This helped unite several fragments. It helps explain why certain children act or react in the way they do.

It seemed to bring everything into perspective and made excellent sense . . . the whole idea and background of collectivism and individualism and why that affects schools . . . I think there is a strong need for this subject in a course such as this.

I have always been interested in the conflict between the individual and society. Thinking America has become too fragmented in subcultures——and individual needs grossly out weigh the collective whole. It clarified and articulated some confusion I have with my Latino friend.

[The model is] very understandable and relevant. Examples were clear and very pertinent. It is helpful in dealing with others——to be aware of

their needs . . . What I liked best was its conciseness of much theory.

## Generativity

From the initial training with the seven elementary school teachers, we learned that "the framework's power lies in the way it generates insights and understanding that enable teachers to bridge cultural differences——the way it gets us questioning, trying to identify for ourselves what social expectations and ethical values are at work" (Trumbull, et al., 2000, p. 4). Would the same be true for teachers–in–training after only one presentation?

### Written Comments

[I will] be more aware of cultural backgrounds and ways of relating to students and parents. [I will] encourage Euro–American children to become more collective and from other cultures more independent with an understanding of both to bring them into a common ground comfortable for both.

[It] Definitely made me think about how to change my approach in the future as teacher and things to be aware of that I would not have thought about.

I teach ESL [English as a Second Language] and find many cultural differences specifically related to individualism and collectivism. [I will] keep my eyes open and be culturally sensitive to my students.

It reinforced some of my common sense suspicions about how knowing a person's culture can aid in teaching them.

I can see new ways to mix my culture with the students and parents.

I will try to practice more collective practices

after having studied it by helping others working in groups.

I'm an extremely individualistic person, many of my students are not. I may try to find ways my students can work together to reinforce each other and work more with the class as a group.

I see the individual attitude I come from and must be mindful of those who come with a different perspective. I can use this model in my classroom and in our family. I would like to study the model further.

### Personal Meaning

Just as awareness is critical to understanding cultural value orientations, making the framework personally meaningful is essential for long–term application. The original seven teachers in the *Bridging Cultures Project* have cited many examples of how the framework was personally meaningful (Rothstein–Fisch, et al., 1997; Trumbull, Diaz–Meza, et al., 2001). Could the same be true of education students after only a three–hour training?

#### *Written Comments*

I could really relate to [the model] because I've been the student having conflict between school and home. It felt good to know that more people thought similar to my upbringing and could actually put [it] into words that made sense to others. I think having the situation explained to us first and seeing the results later was very helpful. [*This person was reared until age 10 in Cuba.*]

It allowed me to understand a specific incident that occurred to me. It will help me analyze my reactions and it will help me analyze my teaching and allow me to be a better teacher. It will help me in my self–reflection enabling me to know

when I'm behaving individualistically and why I react the way I do and why others (students) react in their ways.

It clearly explains the major differences between cultures. I am able to understand why my Mexican–American boyfriend and I thought *so* differently about everything including education. I think it will be extremely helpful when working with children and parents from different backgrounds.

This model will make me look at myself and evaluate, then look at my work and evaluate how I handle myself.

I have been trying to incorporate this kind of model in my work as well as personally. Learning more about it will help me explain it to other people.

I was raised to be individualistic, but I wish I was raised in more of a collectivistic way. I would like to be a bridge——as a teacher, be sensitive to the whole spectrum.

### A Critical Concern

One student had concerns that the model could be misinterpreted or misused:

I don't believe individuals, regardless of their background, neatly fit into each category. I feel I have traits from both individualism and collectivism. I'm sure most people feel this way.

This student saw the framework as a way to dichotomize people rather than as a way to guide understanding of differing cultural value systems. This legitimate concern has been directly addressed and integrated into the current *Module* (see the Preface and the Facilitator's Script), with caveats regarding overgeneralizing the framework explicitly stated.

## Evaluation 2
## Midterm Exam

As part of the midterm exam offered three weeks following presentation of the *Bridging Cultures Module*, students were asked to describe the five most salient parts of the framework. At that time, supplementary readings had not yet been developed to support the learning process; therefore, the responses may contain slight errors that would probably have been corrected if the present *Readings* were available.

Typical responses indicated that students appreciated learning about the differences between individualism and collectivism (n = 12) and conflict between home and school (n = 12), with the recognition that the independent individual need no longer be viewed as the only model for learning and education. The classroom–based examples in the presentation also seemed salient, with students citing the Seven Points of Conflict related to the role of property (n = 9), praise versus criticism (n = 7), parent versus teacher roles (n = 7), emphasis on social role of objects (contextualized) versus cognitive role of objects (decontextualized) (n = 7), independence and interdependence (n = 6), and sharing and helping (n = 6). Overall, students indicated valuing both individualism and collectivism and wrote about their intention to work toward greater harmony between home and school. The full responses that follow are presented in their contextualized format——that is to say, just as the students crafted them. Again, although the responses are persuasive, there are areas where students demonstrate some confusion. This evaluation does not conform to the same pretest, posttest design employed in the original research with the seven in–service elementary school teachers.

## Midterm Descriptions of the Most Salient Parts of *Bridging Cultures*

### Written Comments

I found the BC [*Bridging Cultures*] model to be very insightful. I had not really given much thought to "us vs. them" with regard to how differently our mainstream culture views things as compared to most minority cultures. The following components are ranked in order of importance to me.

1. Individualistic society views the child in school as the parent's responsibility vs. collectivistic cultures viewing it as the teacher's responsibility.
2. Individualistic view of cognitive importance vs. collectivism view of social importance.
3. Individualistic emphasis on independence vs. collectivism's emphasis on interdependence.
4. Individualistic society's use of praise vs. use of criticism by collectivistic societies.
5. Individualistic view of possession of objects vs. importance of sharing in collectivism.

I ranked #1 the most important as it most directly relates to me as a teacher. It's important to know what expectations I should have with regard to homework and other school related activities when it comes to some minorities. I think it will help ease my frustration, and assist me with some possible strategies to "bridge" the gap.

One of the most interesting things I learned from the BC model was the concept of individualism vs. collectivism. The insight into the ways that other cultures think was exciting. The concept of ownership vs. sharing was interesting. Learning in a social context was also new to me. The example of the teacher asking about an egg, and the child starting to tell the story of her grandmother cooking was an important insight for me. Also the saying "the nail that sticks out gets pounded" is so different from the achievement praise orientated way in which I am in. I also thought it was important to be aware of the differences in what the teacher's role is perceived to be. In our society, the teacher is a guide to help children learn. In other societies the teacher is considered to be the authority.

The most important part of the BC model was the way it addressed the differences between collectivism and individualism. I had no idea that the USA was so individualistic, and I did not know the concepts of individualism which are: child seen as individual, personal property, role of parents, and the importance of oral expression. These all create a student [who] is more isolated. I believe that collectivism is more positive. For example, the child is seen as a part of the family, value placed on sharing, helpfulness is positive, it is the teacher's role not parents to teach, and need to respect elders. I believe the most important aspect of [the] BC project will be ways to address how to become more collectivistic in teaching.

The BC model is based on the concept of individualism and collectivism. Individualism involves mainly the viewpoint of white–European thinkers. Collectivism refers to the viewpoint of immigrants. The key points of these view[s] can be stated as follows:
      individual – collective
      child as individual – child as part of the family
      objects belonging to person/school – objects
            for everyone to use
      work independently – work to help group
      teacher as public servant – teacher as
            authority figure
      praise: good self–esteem – criticism: make
            sure the child doesn't stick out.

The most helpful, insightful aspect of *Bridging Cultures* was the way in which Individualist and Collectivist groups view the child. Obviously the Individualist views the child as an individual, but I

had not considered the collectivist view——the child within the context of the family. Secondly, praise to boost self esteem versus the collectivist who will criticize behavior to attain normative behavior. This can be very important to know when meeting a parent and praising (erroneously!) his child when this may be interpreted as non–normal behavior. The notion of ownership versus sharing was a third quality of difference that I had not considered. Your example of [the child] attempting to "share" toys was a vivid reminder of the importance of being aware of this difference.

In order of importance:

(1) most immigrants are collectivistic, (2) we are individualistic, (3) the bridge, (4) the effects of culture on teaching and learning.

The most salient parts of the BC Model are the list of the characteristics of the individualistic and the cooperative [collectivistic] viewpoints. The examples given when the model was presented and the realization of how these differences can affect a student's success in the classroom. They were most salient to me because they were concrete examples of the model. I find myself thinking about the model when I observe behaviors of people from other cultures. What I may have previously considered as "rude" behavior makes more sense now when I look at it from the perspective of the "cooperative" outlook. From most important to least important:
      Possessions vs. sharing;
      Individualism vs. interdependence;
      Cognitive skills vs. social skills;
      Praise vs. criticism;
      Understanding the physical world vs. understanding human relationships.

[The five most salient parts of the framework are:]
      Praise vs. criticism
      independence vs. interdependence

direct exposure vs. human relationships
personal property vs. sharing
individual vs. collective–group

The five most salient parts of *Bridging Cultures*
for me were:
1. I never realized how biased and European
American–based all our teaching is—i.e. our
limited view of the motivating factors that influence and guide learning in other cultures.
2. Individual differences between collectivistic
cultures
3. Our preoccupation with possessions
4. The different family values in our students
5. The enormous benefits we all can achieve
by valuing, accepting, and building upon the
strengths/gifts of various cultures in our
classrooms.

The five most salient parts of the BC model for
me include the awareness that:
1. Immigrant cultures value collectivism vs.
individualism.
2. The conflict that students experience
between home and school values.
3. The meaning and value that collectivism
can contribute to a class.
4. The mainstream value of American education is individualism.
5. The conflicts that can arise in parent–
teacher conferences due to differing social
and learning values.

The most salient points of the BC Framework:
1. The striking differences between collectivism and individualism were very interesting
because the examples were very familiar.
2. The goal of having a deeper awareness of
the differences in cultures and recognizing
that this awareness will affect a teacher's
work in the classroom in a very positive
way.
3. The differences between different cultures

has such an emotional effect on people. I
got this from the example given in class of
the boy who told the girl that what they were
playing with was *his*.
4. It is such a collaborative effort that included
researchers and teachers.
5. I was interested to hear how people answered the beginning problem of the boy
who wasn't feeling well. People had many
different ideas that reflected collectivism and
individualism.

[The five most salient parts of the framework
are:]
individualism vs. collectivism
facts vs. social context learning
private ownership vs. sharing
praise vs. negative criticism
role of the teacher

The most salient point about the BC model for
me is that parents may have far different values
for their children than those that public schools
have traditionally embraced. Once that is understood, it goes on to examine the differences, so I
think that the second important point to remember is that differences do not necessarily imply
that one set of values is more or less worthwhile.
That leads to the third point, namely that teachers must incorporate and accept broader
viewpoints than their own (for example, the girl
when speaking of eggs, segued into a story
about her grandmother). This is of course noth-
ing more than valuing and learning from others.
The fourth point would be the watch, listen, and
ask . . . what is actually transpiring and . . .
whether any intervention is actually necessary.
And fifth, I think children need to be praised for
not only skills representing mainstream values
that they've attained (e.g. cognitive skills and
oral expression) but also for more collectivistic
skills such as respecting authority, sharing and
helpfulness. When a teacher can model a bridge

and accommodate and build on the different cultures in a classroom, I think all the students are enriched.

The most important part of the BC framework was seeing the individualism vs. collectivism disharmony. The idea of understanding physical objects by direct exposure is something I took for granted. I always thought that dealing with an object was the important part. I did not realize that people thought so much about how an object is used in relationships. It is something to consider when asking children to describe what an object is. Also, sharing vs. personal property was interesting. I would think that sharing was just being nice. Being possessive was either hogging something or holding on to needed resources. Why share if you are counting on a resource? Next, praise vs. criticism was very important to learn about. I would think that all praise was good and effective and very little criticism could really be called constructive. It helps my mom and I to better understand how my dad was raised. He was criticized more than praised when in our U.S. culture, we would think that his behavior deserved the reverse. This seems to be linked to independence vs. interdependence. My mom figures that the criticism was my dad's father's way of keeping him, he might feel like deserving independence. This way if he was criticized for not bringing enough money home to his family, he would work even harder so that this family could benefit. As a teacher, I can try to be more aware of how to use praise and criticism. I never knew this was all based on culture and not just the family environment.

The child working for a group vs. themselves is also insightful. At first glance, a child who helps the group is just caring and helpful and the individualistic person is quiet. But, I have learned that a child may be quiet for the group. They do not want to show off because it was not valued to stand out in their culture. When I'm quiet in a class, it is because I may know the answer, but I let others answer and have a chance. I do not consider it based on home culture, but school culture. No one likes the know–it–all kids. I never cared for the show–off.

From this module, I have learned how individualistic I am and my culture is. I have also seen how my dad's Mexican culture is more different than our U.S. ways. Individual vs. collectivistic does not just involve economic positions, as it is the only way I'd considered them before.

## Evaluation 3
## Final Exam

### The Five Most Valuable Things from the Course

Three months after the *Bridging Cultures Module* was presented, 54 students responded to the final exam requirement to "indicate the five most valuable things you learned in the course and cite an application of how this might be applied in your own classroom." The most frequently cited concept in the 15–week course was the *Bridging Cultures* framework, mentioned by 23 students. Students stated that they would apply their knowledge of individualism and collectivism in their work with parents and children, allow for group collaboration, and function with a greater understanding of parental goals. *Bridging Cultures* far exceeded the next two most valuable concepts: Gardner's theory of multiple intelligences (Eggen & Kauchak, 1997) and the role of classroom organization (mentioned 14 times each; see Table 1 for the full set of responses).

It is possible that the students, knowing that their instructor had a personal stake in the framework, inflated the ratings for *Bridging Cultures*. However, informal (and undocumented) class discussions seemed to diminish the likelihood of overinflation because the students routinely discovered new applications of the framework, connecting it to other topics in the course and in their fieldwork placement. In addition, students could have answered the final exam question by using concepts contained in the test itself, drawing on material from the second half of the course as a trigger for their responses. This would not have included the *Bridging Cultures* concepts because it had been presented in the first half of the semester. The course presented a broad view of educational psychology, and the *Bridging Cultures* framework was only a small part of the total course. Other concepts such as developmental theory, learning theory, and reflective practice were central themes throughout the entire course.

In summary, it appears that the *Bridging Cultures* framework (including the theory, research, and field–based examples) was highly valued by teachers–in–training. They were able to envision ways to apply the *Bridging Cultures* framework to their own past experiences as well as the new ones they were encountering or expected to come across as classroom teachers. As with any training, the knowledge and skill of the facilitator (or in this case, professor) are important aspects of the fidelity of implementation. Although we cannot know whether students ended the course with the ability to apply their knowledge to an array of classroom situations, they did seem to respond very favorably to the *Module*. Of course, more follow–up data on the students from these two classes would be ideal, particularly to understand the translation of a three–hour session into direct classroom experiences. However, student teachers are not often afforded the opportunity to shape the prevailing school culture while they are in training, and thus, the long–term effects remain untested and unknown.

In the final evaluation of the *Module*, it does seem that both undergraduates with little teaching experience and graduate students working as emergency–credential teachers found the *Bridging Cultures* framework relevant and useful. Returning to the *Module* objectives, participants were able to:

- Gain awareness and understanding that all people have cultures and no one culture is inherently better than another

- Identify the features of individualism and collectivism

- Examine their own cultural orientations

- Cite examples of home–school conflict

- Describe strategies that apply knowledge of both individualism and collectivism that could help students achieve their full potential

Teachers equipped with models that can inform them of both visible and invisible aspects of culture will truly meet the educational needs of an increasingly diverse student population. The framework of individualism–collectivism has proven helpful in this endeavor, if only to make teachers aware that they themselves operate with cultural value assumptions. Teachers' awareness that this value dimension exists helps them to recognize, understand, respect, and validate a perspective other than their own. Making implicit cultural values visible can prevent the harm to children and families that may arise from conflicts between the values of home and school.

Table 1.   Most Valuable Things Learned
in Psychological Foundations, K–12, Fall, 1997

| Number of responses | Concept |
| --- | --- |
| 23 | *Bridging Cultures* framework of individualism–collectivism. |
| 14 | Classroom organization.  Gardner's theory[1]. |
| 13 | Motivation. |
| 11 | Constructivism. |
| 8 | Assessment: formal/authentic.  Focus on individual needs. Metacognition.  Reflective practice.  Social learning theory. |
| 7 | Developmental models.  Maslow's theory[1].  Steps for effective teaching. |
| 6 | Classroom observations.  Learning contexts and examples.  Use of praise. |
| 5 | Behaviorism.  Piaget[1]. |
| 4 | Bloom's taxonomy[1].  Classroom management.  Communication. High expectations.  Information processing.  Learner–centered classrooms. Meaningfulness.  Open–ended questions.  Scaffolding. |
| 3 | Baseline information on pupils.  Lesson planning.  Problem solving. Rules of discipline.  Successful discussions. |
| 2 | Attitude of teachers.  Classroom rules.  Cooperative learning. Disabled students.  Good feedback.  Wait time. |
| 1 | Attention to learning.  Checking for meaningfulness.  Checking for understanding. Concept webs.  Enthusiasm.  Erikson's theory[1].  Flexibility.  Goal setting. Individual Educational Program for students with special needs. Instructional alignment.  Instructor as a role model.  Learning takes time. Physical health of students.  Role of authority.  Teachers' health.  Test construction. Theories in general.  With–itness (i.e., knowing what is going on in the classroom at all times). |

Note: Students were asked to indicate the five most valuable things they learned on the final exam for the course and to support each with a specific classroom application. (N = 54 respondents with five items each written in essay format.)

[1] Descriptions of these theories were all contained in the course text, Eggen & Kauchak (1997).

*Chapter* 4

# Overhead Transparency Masters

# *Bridging Cultures* Workshop Agenda

- Introduction to the *Bridging Cultures Project*
- Solving a Classroom Dilemma
- Description of the *Bridging Cultures* Framework
- The Seven Points of Home-School Conflict
- Break
- Envisioning the Cultural Bridge
- Questions and Applications
- Evaluation

Rothstein-Fisch, C. *Bridging Cultures Teacher Education Module* (p. 77). Copyright © 2003. Lawrence Erlbaum Associates, Inc.

# The *Bridging Cultures Project*

## Initial training, 1996

Participants

Seven bilingual Spanish-English elementary teachers
(four Latino, three European American)

Method

Three videotaped workshops over four months

Outcome

All teachers learned to understand and apply
the *Bridging Cultures* framework

# The *Bridging Cultures Project*

**Shifting roles, 1997 – 2001**

Bi-monthly meetings provided opportunities to continue applying and researching the framework

Teachers moved from being teacher-participants to teacher-researchers, finding new examples and applications of *Bridging Cultures* in their schools

Teachers became conference presenters, publication co-authors, and school leaders

Rothstein-Fisch, C. *Bridging Cultures Teacher Education Module* (p. 81). Copyright © 2003 Lawrence Erlbaum Associates, Inc.

# Solving a Classroom Dilemma

## The Jobs Scenario

It is the end of the school day, and the class is cleaning up. Salvador isn't feeling well, and he asks Emanuel to help him with his job for the day, which is cleaning the blackboard. Emanuel isn't sure that he will have time to do both jobs.

What do you think the teacher should do?

Rothstein-Fisch, C. (2003). *Bridging Cultures Teacher Education Module* (p. 83). Lawrence Erlbaum Associates, Inc. From Raeff, C., Greenfield, P., Quiroz, B. Conceptualizing interpersonal relationships in the cultural contexts of individualism and collectivism. In S. Harkness, C. Raeff, & C. Super (Eds.), *Variability in the social construction of the child* (pp. 59-74). *New Directions for Child and Adolescent Development*, No. 87. Copyright © 2000 by Wiley. Reprinted with permission.

# Jobs Scenario: School One

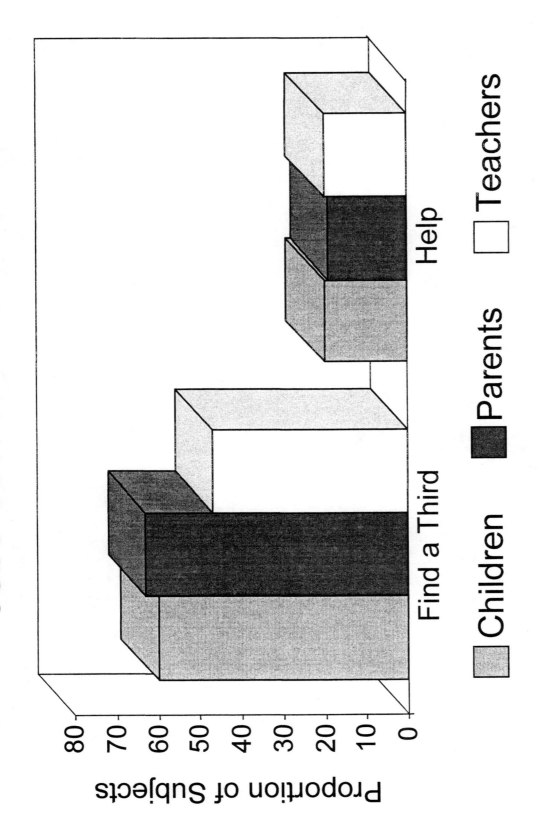

Rothstein-Fisch, C. (2003). *Bridging Cultures Teacher Education Module* (p. 85). Lawrence Erlbaum Associates, Inc. From Raeff, C., Greenfield, P., Quiroz, B. Conceptualizing interpersonal relationships in the cultural contexts of individualism and collectivism. In S. Harkness, C. Raeff, & C. Super (Eds.), *Variability in the social construction of the child* (pp. 59-74). *New Directions for Child and Adolescent Development*, 87. Copyright © 2000 by Wiley. Reprinted with permission.

Overhead 5

# Jobs Scenario: School Two

Legend: Children | Parents | Teachers

X-axis: Find a Third, Help

Y-axis: Proportion of Subjects (0, 10, 20, 30, 40, 50, 60, 70, 80)

Rothstein-Fisch, C. (2003). *Bridging Cultures Teacher Education Module* (p. 87). Lawrence Erlbaum Associates, Inc. From Raeff, C., Greenfield, P., Quiroz, B. Conceptualizing interpersonal relationships in the cultural contexts of individualism and collectivism. In S. Harkness, C. Raeff, & C. Super (Eds.), *Variability in the social construction of the child* (pp. 59-74). *New Directions for Child and Adolescent Development, 87*. Copyright © 2000 by Wiley. Reprinted with permission.

Overhead 6

# The Cost of Home-School Conflict

"[We came to feel that] the rules at school were more important than the rules at home. The school and the teachers were right. As a child, you begin to feel the conflict. Many of my brothers stopped to feel the conflict. Many of my brothers stopped communicating with the family and with my father because he was ignorant."

Amada Irma Pérez
Third-Grade Teacher

Rothstein-Fisch, C. *Bridging Cultures Teacher Education Module* (p. 89). Copyright © 2003. Lawrence Erlbaum Associates, Inc.

# Individualism

**Representative of mainstream U.S. culture**

- Fosters independence and individual achievement

- Emphasizes the physical world, private property, and objects out of context

- Promotes individual needs, self-expression, and personal choice

# Collectivism

**Representative of many immigrant cultures and 70% of the world**

- Fosters interdependence, family, and group success

- Emphasizes the social world, shared property, and objects in social contexts

- Promotes norms, respect for authority and elders, and group consensus

Rothstein-Fisch, C. *Bridging Cultures Teacher Education Module* (p. 91). Copyright © 2003. Lawrence Erlbaum Associates, Inc.

# Hofstede's Individualism Ratings

| | |
|---|---|
| USA | 91 |
| Australia | 90 |
| Great Britain | 89 |
| Canada | 80 |
| Italy | 76 |
| France, Sweden | 71 |
| Germany | 67 |
| Israel | 54 |
| Spain | 51 |
| India | 48 |
| Argentina, Japan | 46 |
| Iran | 41 |
| "Arab countries," Brazil | 38 |
| Philippines | 32 |
| Mexico | 30 |
| "East African countries" | 27 |
| Hong Kong | 25 |
| Singapore, Thailand, "West African countries" | 20 |
| South Korea | 18 |
| Costa Rica | 15 |
| Indonesia, Pakistan | 14 |
| Guatemala | 6 |

# Risk: Overgeneralizing

Socioeconomic status, amount of formal education, and rural or urban origins are powerful predictors of individualism and collectivism.

All cultures, like people, are both individualistic and collectivistic and change over time. However, despite cultural shifts toward the mainstream, child-rearing values can persist over many generations.

# Benefit: Understanding

The individualism-collectivism framework:

- Provides a tool for uncovering cultural variation

- Opens the door for understanding others

- Helps foster meaningful interactions

- Suggests solutions to conflicts

# Seven Sources of Home-School Conflict

## Individualism

- Independence
- Personal property
- Cognitive skills and objects out of context
- Child as individual
- Parents' role to teach
- Praise→positive self-esteem
- Oral expression

## Collectivism

- Helpfulness
- Sharing
- Social skills and objects in social context
- Child as part of a family
- Teacher's role to educate
- Criticize→normative behavior
- Listening to authority

Rothstein-Fisch. C. (2003). *Bridging Cultures Teacher Education Module* (p. 99). Lawrence Erlbaum Associates. Inc. From Trumbull, Rothstein-Fisch, C., & Greenfield, P. M. *Bridging Cultures in Our Schools: New Approaches That Work.* Copyright © 2000 by WestEd. Reprinted with permission.

# Whose Blocks?

Picture this: At preschool, a European American boy was playing with blocks. Nearby, Jasmine, daughter of immigrant Latino parents, took one of the blocks that the boy was not using and began to play with it. In response, the boy hit Jasmine and she began to cry.

What might the teacher think or feel?

What will the teacher do?

# Crayons in the Classroom

A teacher-mentor came to visit a bilingual kindergarten classroom. The mentor observed that the crayons were sorted into cups by color—all the red in one cup, all the blue in another, etc. — and that the class was sharing all the crayons in all the cups.

The mentor suggested putting each child's name on a cup which would contain multicolored crayons which would be used by only that particular child.

Rothstein-Fisch, C. (2003). *Bridging Cultures Teacher Education Module* (p. 103). Lawrence Erlbaum Associates, Inc. From Quiroz, B. & Greenfield, P.M. Cross-cultural value conflict: Removing a barrier to Latino school achievement. In Greenfield, P. M., Isaac, A., Quiroz, B., Rothstein-Fisch, C. Trumbull, E., et al. *Bridging Cultures in Latino Immigrant Education.* Copyright © forthcoming. Russell Sage Foundation, 112 East 64th Street, New York, NY10021. Reprinted with permission.

# Shared School Supplies

# How Would You Describe an Egg?

A kindergarten teacher showed her class an actual chicken egg that would be hatching soon. She explained the physical properties of the egg and asked the children to describe eggs by thinking about the times they had cooked and eaten eggs.

Rothstein-Fisch, C. (2003). *Bridging Cultures Teacher Education Module* (p. 107). Lawrence Erlbaum Associates, Inc. From Greenfield, P. M., Raeff, C., & Quiroz, B. Cultural values in learning and education. In B. Williams (Ed.) *Closing the Achievement Gap: A Vision for Changing Beliefs and Practices* (p. 44). Copyright ©1996 by Association for Supervision and Curriculum Development (www.ascd.org). Reprinted with permission from ASCD. All rights reserved.

# Science from Stories

## Student experience

**Carolina's story**

• Carolina was playing in the garden with her grandmother

• She saw a hummingbird near the cherry tree

• It "stood in the air"

• Carolina tried to get close to the pretty bird, but it kept moving away

## Scientific information

**Hummingbird qualities**

• Brownish with bright irides-cent green and red coloring around head and neck

• Wings beat rapidly

• Can hover, fly in any direction

• Must eat frequently because constant energy is required for movements

Overhead 17

# School Breakfast

There had just been a major crisis involving the federally funded school breakfast program. The problem, as seen by the school, was that immigrant Latina mothers were accompanying their children to school, bringing younger siblings, and eating the school breakfast together with their children; as a consequence, eating food that "belonged" only to the school children.

# School Sign

ONLY STUDENTS ARE PERMITTED IN EATING AREA

SOLAMENTE SE PERMITEN A ESTUDIANTES EN LA AREA DE COMER

United School District
**_Greenfield Elementary School_**
448 Ninth Street, Greenfield, CA 90000

C. Alena
_Superintendent of Schools_

Brenda Steppes
_Principal_

November 3, 1997

Dear Greenfield Parents:

As many of you know our school is a closed-campus school. This was decided after incidents which we felt could put the children in danger. The entrance for adults in our school is the main door on Eighth Street. This helps the office and other personnel keep track of adults on campus. It also limits strangers or others from coming into school by closing down all other gates.

In addition, federal regulations prohibit us from allowing anyone other than registered school students in the lunch area. We receive a free meal program schoolwide and the rules are that these meals are to be served only to students. Unfortunately, sitting with your child in the lunch area could cause us to lose this privilege. Losing this privilege would mean that your child's breakfast would cost $ .60 and lunch $ .85 a day for a total of $7.25 a week per child. The other option would be to have each child bring his/her own meals.

Please understand that we are enforcing these rules in order to keep our campus safe and our meal program fee.

All parents are welcome to get involved in our school activities and we also encourage you to visit our parent center for more information about our parent services.

Thank you in advance for your cooperation and understanding in these matters.

Sincerely,

Brenda Steppes
Principal

# Parents' Role versus Teacher's Role

In a study of immigrant Latino families, Valdés found that mothers "saw themselves as participating actively in their children's *educación*, that is, in raising children to be good and well-behaved human beings. They did not, however, see themselves as adjunct schoolteachers. They did not see their role as involving the teaching of school subjects. In their own experience in school, this had been the province of the teacher."

# Group Homework Practice

# Praise versus Criticism

A Mexican immigrant mother recalls her experience in a parent-teacher conference in which her child's teacher called her daughter "outstanding." According to this mother, "I did not know what to do about her being 'outstanding': I had tried to show my daughter not to 'show off' or be cruel to others, but it seemed it was not working. I blamed her 'bad habit' of 'standing out' on this country's social influences as I had seen on TV and in my personal observations."

Rothstein-Fisch, C. (2003). *Bridging Cultures Teacher Education Module* (p. 121). Lawrence Erlbaum Associates, Inc. From Quiroz, B. & Greenfield, P.M. Cross-cultural value conflict: Removing a barrier to Latino school achievement. In Greenfield, P. M., Isaac, A., Quiroz, B. Rothstein-Fisch, C. Trumbull, E., et al. *Bridging Cultures in Latino Immigrant Education*. Copyright © forthcoming. Russell Sage Foundation, 112 East 64th Street, New York, NY10021. Reprinted with permission.

# Oral Expression versus Respect for Authority

In individualistic cultures, it is often said that "the squeaky wheel gets the grease."

In collectivistic cultures, it's often said that "the nail that sticks up gets pounded down"!

Rothstein-Fisch, C. (2003). *Bridging Cultures Teacher Education Module* (p. 123). Lawrence Erlbaum Associates, Inc.

# Guilt in the Principal's Office

# You Are the Bridge

Envision that you are building a cultural bridge.

• What does the bridge connect?

• How long and wide would it be?

• What materials would be used to construct the bridge and who would build it?

• What would the bridge look like?

Draw the bridge.

*Chapter* **5**

# Handout Templates

## HANDOUT 1
## Solving a Classroom Dilemma: The Jobs Scenario

A "scenario" is a brief vignette. This one demonstrates how differing value orientations lead to different interpretations of the same event or of different behaviors in the same circumstances.

> It is the end of the school day, and the class is cleaning up. Salvador isn't feeling well, and he asks Emanuel to help him with his job for the day, which is cleaning the blackboard. Emanuel isn't sure that he will have time to do both jobs.

> What do you think the teacher should do?

Rothstein-Fisch, C. (2003). *Bridging Cultures Teacher Education Module* (p. 131). Lawrence Erlbaum Associates, Inc. From: Raeff, C., Greenfield, P. M., & Quiroz, B. (2000). Conceptualizing interpersonal relationships in the cultural contexts of individualism and collectivism. In S. Harkness, C. Raeff, & C. Super (Eds.), Variability in the social construction of the child, *New Directions for Child and Adolescent Development*, 2000 (87), 66. Copyright © 2000 by Jossey-Bass Publishers. Reprinted with permission. See *Readings* Article 5.

# HANDOUT 2
## Seven Sources of Home–School Conflict

### 1. Independence versus Helpfulness

Example: Should a student help a sick friend clean the chalkboard? Data reveal that parents and children from immigrant Latino families solved this problem differently from European American families.

Application: Allow students to help each other by suggesting several monitors to get a classroom job done or use the whole group to help. Allow students to assist each other with academic work.

*Notes:*

### 2. Personal property versus Sharing

Example: Sharing blocks or crayons may be more natural for some students than maintaining personal temporary ownership of classroom materials.

Application: Encourage students to share. Be clear that although materials belong to the whole class, in some instances it might be appropriate to ask permission to use certain ones.

*Notes:*

Rothstein-Fisch, C. (2003). *Bridging Cultures Teacher Education Module* (p. 133). Lawrence Erlbaum Associates, Inc.
See: Trumbull, E., Rothstein-Fisch, C., & Greenfield, P. M. *Bridging Cultures in our Schools: New Approaches that Work.*
Copyright © 2000 by WestEd. Reprinted with permission. See: *Readings* Article 1.

3. **Cognitive skills and objects out of context versus Social skills and objects in a social context**

Example:       Having children share their stories about real life experiences (such as with hummingbirds) connects their lived experiences with cognitive concepts.

Application:  Encourage students to share stories as valuable in themselves as well as being starting points for connecting lived experiences with academic topics.

*Notes:*

4. **Child as an individual versus Child as part of the family**

Example:       Federal regulations prohibiting family members from sitting with their children during subsidized meals caused a crisis because families were accustomed to eating together. Likewise, parents sought to maintain the family as a unit rather than discussing only one child during parent–teacher conferences.

Application:  When nonnegotiable school policies conflict with families' prevailing values, offer clear explanations as to why the policies exist and welcome parents' participation and involvement in meaningful, sincere, and sustaining ways. During parent–teacher conferences, ask about the well–being of the whole family.

*Notes:*

Rothstein-Fisch, C. (2003). *Bridging Cultures Teacher Education Module* (p. 133). Lawrence Erlbaum Associates, Inc. See: Trumbull, E., Rothstein-Fisch, C., & Greenfield, P. M. *Bridging Cultures in our Schools: New Approaches that Work.* Copyright © 2000 by WestEd. Reprinted with permission. See: *Readings* Article 1.

## 5. Parents' role to teach versus Teacher's role to educate

Example:    Teachers often expect parents to teach academic subjects at home, whereas collectivistic parents may believe that academic instruction is strictly the role of the teacher.

Application:    Establish realistic homework practices (that might include homework practice in class) and possibly rethink student–led conferences in favor of group parent conferences.

*Notes:*

## 6. Praise versus Criticism

Example:    Praise is often used as a way to encourage students, but it backfired when immigrant Latino students felt it was insincere.

Application:    Using praise in private and in specific ways such as "interesting word choice" or "well–punctuated" is helpful. Praise may work best for the whole class, so as not to single out any one student. Encourage students to ask themselves, "Is this my best work?"

*Notes*

Rothstein-Fisch, C. (2003). *Bridging Cultures Teacher Education Module* (p. 133). Lawrence Erlbaum Associates, Inc. See: Trumbull, E., Rothstein-Fisch, C., & Greenfield, P. M. *Bridging Cultures in our Schools: New Approaches that Work.* Copyright © 2000 by WestEd. Reprinted with permission. See: *Readings* Article 1.

## 7. Oral expression versus Listening to authority

Example:    Because he did not speak up or look the principal in the eye in his own defense, a student was believed to be guilty of a school–related crime. Some students learn better by listening with respect compared to speaking out in class.

Application:    Support listening to and respect for authority. Offer a variety of speaking options, including one–on–one, choral responses, small groups, and whole group.

*Notes:*

Rothstein-Fisch, C. (2003). *Bridging Cultures Teacher Education Module* (p. 133). Lawrence Erlbaum Associates, Inc. See: Trumbull, E., Rothstein-Fisch, C., & Greenfield, P. M. *Bridging Cultures in our Schools: New Approaches that Work.* Copyright © 2000 by WestEd. Reprinted with permission. See: *Readings* Article 1.

# HANDOUT 3
## You Are the Bridge

Envision a cultural bridge.

1. What does the bridge connect?

2. How long and wide would it be?

3. What materials would be used to construct the bridge and who would build it?

4. What would the bridge look like?

Now, draw the bridge you see.

# HANDOUT 4
## *Bridging Cultures* Teacher Education Module Evaluation

1. What are the most helpful ideas or insights you gained from the *Bridging Cultures* presentation and why are they useful?

a)

b)

c)

2. What suggestions do you have to improve this presentation?

3. How will you use what you learned about *Bridging Cultures* in your work?

Rate the session overall:

| 5 | 4 | 3 | 2 | 1 |
|---|---|---|---|---|
| very informative | | somewhat informative | | not informative |

Name (optional but useful):

Your story: Describe one experience you have had that might be explained by the framework of individualism and collectivism. Tell the story of what happened and how cultural values might have been in conflict. Give as much detail as possible. Feel free to add additional paper.

# Appendices

## APPENDIX 1 *Bridging Cultures Project* Participants

### Core Researchers

| | |
|---|---|
| Patricia Greenfield | Department of Psychology<br>University of California, Los Angeles |
| Blanca Quiroz | Graduate School of Education<br>Harvard University |
| Carrie Rothstein-Fisch | Michael D. Eisner College of Education<br>California State University, Northridge |
| Elise Trumbull | Culture and Language in Education<br>WestEd |

### Teacher Participants

| | |
|---|---|
| Marie Altchech<br>Stoner Avenue School | Los Angeles Unified School District |
| Catherine Daley<br>Magnolia Elementary School | Los Angeles Unified School District |
| Kathryn Eyler<br>Hoover Elementary School | Los Angeles Unified School District |
| Elvia Hernandez<br>Griffin Avenue Elementary School | Los Angeles Unified School District |
| Giancarlo Mercado<br>Westminster Avenue School | Los Angeles Unified School District |
| Amada Pérez<br>Mar Vista Elementary School | Ocean View School District<br>Oxnard, CA |
| Pearl Saitzyk<br>Westminster Avenue School | Los Angeles Unified School District |

## APPENDIX 2 The Hofstede Study and Expanded Data Set

Discussions of cultural value systems often raise a question about countries of origin: To what degree are ancestral countries individualistic or collectivistic? Overhead 9 includes a partial list of countries and regions studied by Geert Hofstede (1980, 1983, 2001), but participants may ask about other countries. Therefore, a complete list of the countries and regions studied by Hofstede is included to help answer the question, "How individualistic or collectivistic is my country of origin?"

The Hofstede (2001) study is described here very briefly, followed by some important warnings about misinterpreting the data. As participants look at the list of their home countries or their ancestor's native countries, remind them that they are seeing an index of individualism. Encourage them to calculate the complementary collectivism index—subtracting the individualism score from 100—and ask them how this might relate to their own cultural values system.

## The Hofstede Study

Between 1966 and 1978, a large multinational business corporation (IBM, International Business Machines) employed social psychologist Geert Hofstede. While working in the European headquarters, he noticed how people from a variety of countries and regions behaved differently in the same situations, despite common company rules. He also noticed that he and his family interacted differently with schools compared to indigenous families. He gathered a vast array of data from paper–and–pencil surveys of employees, covering 72 countries twice, in 1968 and 1972.

The survey questions tapped employee values and beliefs. Taking the cultural value system as a whole within a country, Hofstede (1980, 1983, 2001) distilled four dimensions:

1. Power distance: The extent to which a society accepts power being unequally distributed.

2. Uncertainty avoidance: The level of discomfort members of a society experience when faced with ambiguous situations.

3. Masculinity: The degree to which a society sees sharp sex role differences.

4. "*Individualism* on the one side versus its opposite, *collectivism* is the degree to which individuals are supposed to look after themselves or remain integrated into groups, usually around the family." (Hofstede, 2001, p. xx)

Some important cautions should accompany the interpretation of Hofstede's work (1980, 1983, 2001). First, the research has been criticized for not providing an adequate representation of each country, and it is likely that the original studies may already have been skewed toward individualism because a large corporation would require personnel to work in urban areas rather than rural regions where collectivism is more prominent. Hofstede (2001) responds, "The country scores obtained correlated highly with all kinds of other data, including results from representative samples of entire national populations" (p. 73). However, the methods used assumed reasonably high levels of literacy and do not represent the immigrant families targeted in the *Module*. Second, there has also been a shift toward greater individualism associated with increases in national wealth. What would scores look like now? Third, would there be differences among the countries grouped by regions? Most important, the data reported is based on countries or regions, not on how any single individual responded to questions about values and beliefs.

## Hofstede's Values for Fifty Countries and Three Regions

The "Index of Individualism" is how each country or region was rated on a scale from 0 to 100, from least individualistic to most individualistic (listed in alphabetical order).

Regions grouped as aggregate data in the original study were: East Africa (Ethiopia, Kenya, Tanzania, Zambia) 27; West Africa (Ghana, Nigeria, Sierra Leone) 20 ; and Arab Countries (Egypt, Iraq, Kuwait, Lebanon, Libya, Saudi Arabia, United Arab Emirates) 38.

## Table 2. Index of Individualism

| | | | | | |
|---|---|---|---|---|---|
| Arab countries | 38 | Guatemala | 6 | Peru | 16 |
| Argentina | 46 | Hong Kong | 25 | Philippines | 32 |
| Australia | 90 | Indonesia | 14 | Portugal | 27 |
| Austria | 55 | India | 48 | South Africa | 65 |
| Belgium | 75 | Iran | 41 | Salvador | 19 |
| Brazil | 38 | Ireland | 70 | Singapore | 20 |
| Canada | 80 | Israel | 54 | Spain | 51 |
| Chile | 23 | Italy | 76 | Sweden | 71 |
| Columbia | 13 | Jamaica | 39 | Switzerland | 68 |
| Costa Rica | 15 | Japan | 46 | Taiwan | 17 |
| Denmark | 74 | Korea (South) | 18 | Thailand | 20 |
| East Africa countries | 27 | Malaysia | 26 | Turkey | 37 |
| Ecuador | 8 | Mexico | 30 | Uruguay | 36 |
| Finland | 63 | Netherlands | 80 | United States | 91 |
| France | 71 | Norway | 69 | Venezuela | 12 |
| Germany | 67 | New Zealand | 79 | West Africa countries | 20 |
| Great Britain | 89 | Pakistan | 14 | Yugoslavia | 27 |
| Greece | 35 | Panama | 11 | | |

Note: From Hofstede, 2001, p. 215.

# References

Banks, J. A. (1997). *Teaching strategies for ethnic studies* (3rd ed.). Boston: Allyn & Bacon.

Banks, J. A. (2001). *Cultural diversity and education: Foundations, curriculum, and teaching* (4th. ed). Boston: Allyn & Bacon.

Brislin, R., & Yoshida, T. (1994). *Intercultural communication training: An introduction.* Thousand Oaks, CA: Sage.

*California State University, Northridge Undergraduate/Graduate Catalog.* (1996–1998). Northridge, CA: California State University, Northridge.

Derman–Sparks, L., & Philips, C. B. (1997*). Teaching/learning anti–racism: A developmental approach.* New York: Teachers College Press.

Eggen, P., & Kauchak, D. (1994). *Educational psychology: Windows on classrooms.* Upper Saddle River, NJ: Merrill.

Finkelstein, B., Pickert, S., Mahoney, T., & Barry, D. (1998). *Discovering culture in education: An approach to cultural education program evaluation.* Washington, DC: ERIC Clearinghouse on Assessment and Evaluation.

Geary, J. P. (2001). *Bridging Cultures through school counseling: Theoretical understanding and practical solutions.* Unpublished master's thesis, California State University, Northridge, Department of Educational Psychology and Counseling.

Girard, K., & Koch, S. J. (1996). *Conflict resolution in the schools: A manual for educators.* San Francisco: Jossey–Bass.

Goldenberg, C., & Gallimore, R. (1995). Immigrant Latino parents' values and beliefs about their children's education: Continuities and discontinuities across cultures and generations. *Advances in Motivational and Achievement*, 9, 183–228.

Greenfield, P. M. (1994). Interdependence and interdependence as developmental scripts: Implications for theory, research, and practice. In P. M. Greenfield & R. R. Cocking (Eds.), *Cross–cultural roots of minority child development* (pp. 1–37). Mahwah, NJ: Lawrence Erlbaum Associates, Inc.

Greenfield, P. M., & Cocking, R. R. (Eds.). (1994). *Cross–cultural roots of minority child development*. Mahwah, NJ: Lawrence Erlbaum Associates, Inc.

Greenfield, P. M., Quiroz, B., & Raeff, C. (2000). Cross–cultural conflict and harmony in the social construction of the child. *New directions for child and adolescent development*, 2000 (87), 93–108.

Greenfield, P. M., Raeff, C., & Quiroz, B. (1996). Cultural values in learning and education. In B. Williams (Ed.), *Closing the achievement gap: A vision for changing beliefs and practices* (pp. 37–55). Alexandria, VA: Association for Supervision and Curriculum Development.

Greenfield, P. M., Rothstein–Fisch, C., & Quiroz, B. (2000, April). *Cross–cultural values in the education of immigrant Mexican and South American children.* Paper presented at the meeting of the American Educational Research Association, New Orleans, LA.

Greenfield, P. M., & Suzuki, L. K. (1998). Culture and human development: Implications for parenting, education, pediatrics, and mental health. In W. Damon (Ed.), I. E. Siegel & K. A. Renninger (Vol. Eds.), *Handbook of child psychology*: 5th ed., Vol. 4 (pp. 1059–1109). New York: Wiley.

Gudykunst, W. B. (1994). *Bridging differences: Effective intergroup communication.* (2nd ed.) Thousand Oaks, CA: Sage.

Guerra, P. L., & Garcia, S. B. (2000*). Understanding the cultural contexts of teaching and learning: A training guide.* Austin, TX: Southwest Educational Development Laboratory.

Hale–Benson, J. E. (1986). *Black children: Their roots, culture, and learning styles.* Baltimore: Johns Hopkins University Press.

Hofstede, G. (1980). *Culture's consequences: International differences in work–related values.* Beverly Hills, CA: Sage.

Hofstede, G. (1983). National cultures revisited. *Behavioral Science Research*, 18, 285–305.

Hofstede. G. (2001). *Culture's consequences: Comparing values, behaviors, institutions, and organizations across nations* (2nd ed.). Thousand Oaks, CA: Sage

Joint Commission to Develop a Master Plan for Education (2002). *The California Master Plan for Education.* Retrieved December 18, 2002, from http://www.sen.ca.gov/masterplan/020909 themasterplanlinks.html

Kohn, A. (1993). *Punished by rewards.* Boston: Houghton Mifflin.

Ladson–Billings, G. (1994). *The dreamkeepers: Successful teachers of African American children.* San Francisco: Jossey–Bass.

Lambert, W. F., Hammers, J. F., & Frasure–Smith, N. (1979). *Child rearing values: A cross–national study.* New York: Praeger.

Lustig, M. W., & Koester, J. (1999*). Intercultural competence: Interpersonal communication across cultures* (3rd ed.). New York: Addison–Wesley–Longman.

Mesa–Bains, A., & Shulman, J. H. (1994). Diversity in the classroom: Facilitator's guide. Hillsdale, NJ: Lawrence Erlbaum Associates, Inc.

Moles, O. C. (Ed.). (1996). *Reaching all families: Creating family–friendly schools.* Washington, DC: Office of Educational Research and Improvement.

National Educational Goals Panel (2000). *Promising practices: Progress from the Goals 2000, Lessons from the states.* Retrieved July 29, 2002, from http://www.negp.gov/promprac/ promprac00/promprac00.pdf

Quiroz, B., & Greenfield, P. M. (forthcoming). Cross–cultural value conflict: Removing a barrier to Latino school achievement. In P.M. Greenfield, A. Isaac, B. Quiroz, C. Rothstein–Fisch, & E. Trumbull (Eds.). *Bridging cultures in Latino immigrant education.* New York, Russell Sage Foundation.

Quiroz, B., Greenfield, P. M., & Altchech, M. (1999). *Bridging Cultures* with a parent–teacher conference. *Educational Leadership*, 56(7), 68–70.

Raeff, C., Greenfield, P. M., & Quiroz, B. (2000). Conceptualizing interpersonal relationships in the cultural contexts of individualism and collectivism. *New directions for child and adolescent development*, 2000(87), 93–108.

Rothstein–Fisch, C. (1998). Bridging cultures: A pre–service teacher training module. San Francisco: WestEd.

Rothstein–Fisch, C. (2000). [Compendium of interviews with the *Bridging Cultures* Teachers]. Unpublished raw data.

Rothstein–Fisch, C., Greenfield, P. M., & Trumbull, E. (1999). Bridging cultures with classroom strategies. *Educational Leadership*, 56(7), 64–67.

Rothstein–Fisch, C., Quiroz, B., Daley, C., & Mercado, G. (1997, July). *Bridging cultures: Conflict prevention through cross–cultural understanding*. Paper presented at the Conflict–Resolution Network Conference, Irving, TX.

Rothstein–Fisch, C., Trumbull, E., Quiroz, B., & Greenfield, P. (1997, June). *Bridging cultures in the schools*. Poster session presented at the Jean Piaget Society Conference, Santa Monica, CA.

Rothstein–Fisch, C., Trumbull, E., Isaac, A., Daley, C., & Pérez, A. (2001, April). *When helping someone else is the right answer: The* Bridging Cultures Project. Paper presented at the meeting of the American Educational Research Association, Seattle, WA.

Singelis, T. M. (Ed.). (1998). *Teaching about culture, ethnicity and diversity: Exercises and planned activities*. Thousand Oaks, CA: Sage.

Triandis, H. C. (1989). Cross–cultural studies of individualism and collectivism. *Nebraska Symposium on Motivation, 37*, 41–133.

Trumbull, E., Diaz–Meza, R., Hasan, A., & Rothstein–Fisch, C. (2001*). The* Bridging Cultures Project *Five–Year Report*, 1996–2000. Retrieved July 29, 2001 from http://www.wested.org/ bridging/BC_5yr_report.pdf.

Trumbull, E., Rothstein–Fisch, C., & Greenfield, P. M. (2000*). Bridging cultures in our schools: New approaches that work*. San Francisco: WestEd.

Trumbull, E., Rothstein–Fisch, C., Greenfield, P. M., & Quiroz, B. (2001). Bridging Cultures *between home and school: A guide for teachers*. Mahwah, NJ: Lawrence Erlbaum Associates, Inc.

Valdés, G. (1996). Con respeto*: Bridging the distances between culturally diverse families and schools, an ethnographic portrait*. New York: Teachers College Press.

# Author Index

## A

Altchech xii, 12

## B

Banks 1
Barry x
Brislin xi, 53, 64

## C

Cocking x, 2, 4

## D

Daley 27
Derman–Sparks 8

## E

Eggen 71, 73

## F

Finkelstein x, 10
Frasure–Smith 5

## G

Garcia xi, 53, 64
Geary 64
Girard 10
Greenfield ix, x, xii, xiv,1, 2, 4, 5, 8, 12,
    13, 25, 26, 29, 31, 32, 33, 34, 36, 38,
    39, 42, 43, 46, 48
Gudykunst ix
Guerra xi, 53, 64

## H

Hale–Benson x
Hasan xi, 4, 5, 13
Hofstede xii, 21, 22, 23, 151, 152

**J**

Joint Committee to Develop a Master Plan  62

**K**

Kauchak  71, 73
Koch  10
Koester  xi, 53
Kohn  50

**L**

Ladson–Billings  x
Lambert  5, 25
Lustig  xi, 53

**M**

Mahoney  x
Mesa–Bains  9
Moles  62

**N**

National Education Goals Panel  59

**P**

Pérez  27
Philips  8
Pickert  x

**Q**

Quiroz  ix, xii, xiii, xiv, 1, 2, 4, 5, 12, 13,
    15, 26, 29, 31, 32, 33, 38, 39, 42, 43,
    45, 46, 48

**R**

Raeff  ix, xii, 1, 4, 12, 17, 42, 43, 46
Rothstein–Fisch  xi, xii, xiii, xiv, 1, 2, 4, 5,
    8, 13, 15, 27, 34, 36, 41, 46, 54, 55,
    67

**S**

Singelis  xi
Suzuki  5, 25, 38

**T**

Triandis  xi, xii, xiv, 22
Trumbull  1, 2, 4, 5, 8, 12, 13, 15, 27, 46,
    52, 66, 67

**V**

Valdés  25, 45, 46

**Y**

Yoshida  53, 64